Autodesk
# AutoCAD Architecture 2008
# Fundamentals

## Elise Moss

ISBN: 978-1-58503-358-4

PUBLICATIONS

**Schroff Development Corporation**

**www.schroff.com**
www.schroff-europe.com

## Schroff Development Corporation
P.O. Box 1334
Mission, KS 66222
(913) 262-2664
www.schroff.com

**Trademarks**

The following are registered trademarks of Autodesk, Inc.: AutoCAD, Architectural Desktop, Inventor, Autodesk, AutoLISP, AutoCAD Design Center, Autodesk Device Interface, and HEIDI.

Microsoft, Windows, NetMeeting, Word, and Excel are either registered trademarks or trademarks of Microsoft Corporation.

All other trademarks are trademarks of their respective holders.

**Copyright 2007 by Elise Moss**

Moss, Elise
    Autodesk AutoCAD Architecture 2008 Fundamentals
    Elise Moss
ISBN: 978-1-58503-358-4 (book only)
ISBN: 978-1-58503-359-1 (book plus software)

The author and publisher of this book have used their best efforts in preparing this book. These efforts include the development, research, and testing of material presented. The author and publisher shall not be held liable in any event for incidental or consequential damages with, or arising out of, the furnishing, performance, or use of the material herein.

**Examination Copies:**

Books received as examination copies are for review purposes only and may not be made available for student use. Resale of examination copies is prohibited.

**Electronic Files:**

Any electronic files associated with this book are licensed to the original user only. These files may not be transferred to any other party.

Printed and bound in the United States of America.

# Also by Elise Moss:

**ISBN: 978-1-58503-344-7**

**551 pages**

# Autodesk AutoCAD 2008:
# Fundamentals

This is a basic training course for new AutoCAD users. It is geared for students with little or no prior experience using AutoCAD. The book covers fundamental skills necessary for effectively using AutoCAD and will provide a strong foundation for advancement.

## Table of Contents

**Download a sample chapter and the complete table of contents from:**
# www.schroff.com

# Preface

For users familiar with Architectural Desktop, the 2008 release of AutoCAD Architecture marks a serious advance in the software's features. No textbook can cover all the features in any software application. This textbook is meant for beginning users who want to gain a familiarity with the tools and interface of AutoCAD Architecture before they start exploring on their own. By the end of the text, users should feel comfortable enough to create a standard model, and even know how to customize the interface for their own use. Knowledge of basic AutoCAD and its commands is helpful, but not required. I do try to explain as I go, but for the sake of brevity I concentrate on the tools specific to and within AutoCAD Architecture.

The files used in this text are accessible from the Internet at www.schroff1.com/. They are free and available to students and teachers alike.

We value customer input. Please contact us with any comments, questions, or concerns about this text.

Elise Moss
elise_moss@mossdesigns.com

# Acknowledgements from Elise Moss

This book would not have been possible without the support of some key Autodesk employees. I especially appreciate the heads-up as to the change of the software name from Architectural Desktop to AutoCAD Architecture. I still am not clear as to why the break from AutoCAD Electrical and AutoCAD Mechanical, but I am sure the marketing whizzes at Autodesk have their reasons.


The effort and support of the editorial and production staff of Schroff Development Corporation is gratefully acknowledged. I especially thank Stephen Schroff for his helpful suggestions regarding the format of this text.

Finally, truly infinite thanks to Ari for his encouragement and his faith.

- Elise Moss

# TABLE OF CONTENTS

## Lesson 1:
# Desktop Features

AutoCAD Architecture (AUTOCAD ARCHITECTURE) enlists object oriented process systems (OOPS). That means that AUTOCAD ARCHITECTURE uses intelligent objects to create a building. This is similar to using blocks in AutoCAD. Objects in AutoCAD Architecture are blocks on steroids. They have intelligence already embedded into them. A wall is not just a collection of lines. It represents a real wall. It can be constrained, has thickness and material properties, and is automatically included in your building schedule.

AEC is an acronym for Architectural/Electrical/Construction.
BID is an acronym for Building Industrial Design.
AIA is an acronym for the Architectural Association in America.

The following table describes the key features of objects in AutoCAD Architecture:

| Feature Type | Description |
|---|---|
| AEC Camera | Create perspective views from various camera angles. Create avi files. |
| AEC Profiles | Create AEC objects using polylines to build doors, windows, etc. |
| Anchors and Layouts | Define a spatial relationship between objects. Create a layout of anchors on a curve or a grid to set a pattern of anchored objects, such as doors or columns. |
| Annotation | Set up special arrows, leaders, bar scales. |
| Ceiling Grids | Create reflected ceiling plans with grid layouts. |
| Column Grids | Define rectangular and radial building grids with columns and bubbles. |
| Design Center | Customize your AEC block library. |
| Display System | Control views for each AEC object. |
| Doors and Windows | Create custom door and window styles or use standard objects provided with the software. |
| Elevations and Sections | An elevation is basically a section view of a floor plan. |
| Layer Manager | Create layer standards based on AIA CAD Standards. Create groups of layers. Manage layers intelligently using Layer Filters. |
| Masking Blocks | Store a mask using a polyline object and attach to AEC objects to hide graphics. |
| Model Explorer | View a model and manage the content easily. Attach names to mass elements to assist in design. |
| Multi-view blocks | Blocks have embedded defined views to allow you to easily change view. |

| Feature Type | Description |
|---|---|
| Railings | Create or apply different railing styles to a stair or along a defined path |
| Roofs | Create and apply various roof styles. |
| Floorplate slices | Generate the perimeter geometry of a building. |
| Spaces and Boundaries | Spaces and boundaries can include floor thickness, room height, and wall thickness. |
| Stairs | Create and apply various stair types |
| Tags and Schedules | Place tags on objects to generate schedules. Schedules will automatically update when tags are modified, added, or deleted. |
| Template Files | Use templates to save time. Create a template with standard layers, text styles, linetypes, dimension styles, etc. |
| Walls | Create wall styles to determine material composition. Define end caps to control opening and end conditions. Define wall interference conditions. |

AutoCAD Architecture sits on top of AutoCAD. It is helpful for users to have a basic understanding of AutoCAD before moving to AutoCAD Architecture. Users should be familiar with the following:

- AutoCAD toolbars
- zoom and move around the screen
- manage blocks
- draw and modify commands
- model and paper space (layout),
- dimensioning and how to create/modify a dimension style

If you are not familiar with these topics, you can still move forward with learning AutoCAD Architecture, but you may find it helpful to have a good AutoCAD textbook as reference in case you get stuck.

**TIP:** The best way to use AutoCAD Architecture is start your project with massing tools (outside-in design) or space planning tools (inside-out design) and continue through to construction documentation.

## *The AEC Project Process Model*

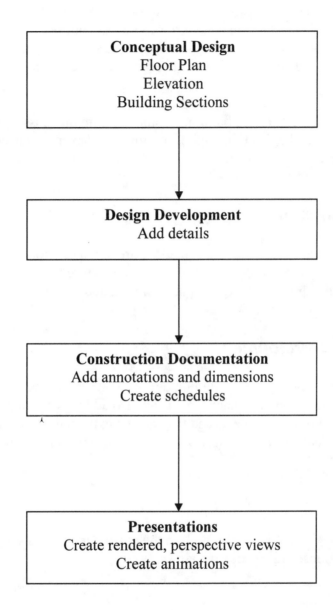

## Conceptual Design

In the initial design phase, you can assemble AutoCAD Architecture mass elements as simple architectural shapes to form an exterior model of your building project. You can also lay out interior areas by arranging general spaces as you would in a bubble diagram. You can manipulate and consolidate three-dimensional mass elements into massing studies.

Later in this phase, you can create building footprints from the massing study by slicing floorplates, and you can begin defining the structure by converting space boundaries into walls. At the completion of the conceptual design phase, you have developed a workable schematic floor plan.

## Design Development

As you refine the building project, you can add more detailed information to the schematic design. Use the features in AutoCAD Architecture to continue developing the design of the building project by organizing, defining, and assigning specific styles and attributes to building components.

## Construction Development

After you have fully developed the building design, you can annotate your drawings with reference marks, notes, and dimensions. You can also add tags or labels associated with objects. Information from the objects and tags can be extracted, sorted, and compiled into schedules, reports, tables, and inventories for comprehensive and accurate construction documentation.

## Presentations

A major part of any project is presenting it to the customer. At this stage, you develop renderings, animations, and perspective views.

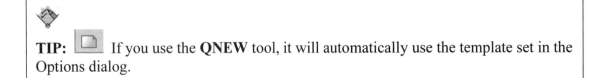

**TIP:** If you use the **QNEW** tool, it will automatically use the template set in the Options dialog.

*Exercise 1-1:*
## Setting the Template for QNEW

Drawing Name:     New
Estimated Time:     15 minutes

This exercise reinforces the following skills:

- Use of templates
- Getting the user familiar with tools and the AUTOCAD ARCHITECTURE environment

1.   Launch AUTOCAD ARCHITECTURE.

2.   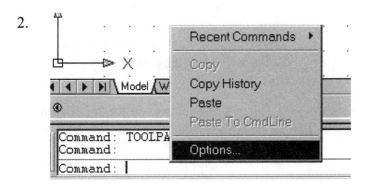 Place your cursor on the command line.

Right click the mouse.

Select **Options** from the short-cut menu.

3.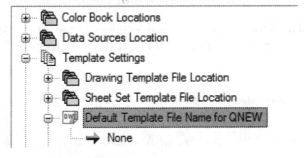

Select the **Files** tab.
Locate the Template Settings folder.
Click on the + symbol to expand.
Locate the Default Template File Name for QNEW.

4.   Browse...   Highlight the path and file name listed and select the **Browse** button.

5.

Local Disk (C:)
Documents and Settings
All Users
Application Data
Autodesk
ADT
enu
Template

Browse to the *Template* folder.

This should be listed under *Documents & Settings\[user name]\Local Settings\Application Data\Autodesk\ADT 2008\enu...*

6.

File name: | Aec Model (Imperial Ctb).dwt

Files of type: | Template File (*.dwt)

Locate the *Aec Model (Imperial Ctb).dwt* file.

Press **Open**.

7.

Template Settings
Drawing Template File Location

Note that you can also set where you can direct the user for templates. This is useful if you want to create standard templates and place them on networks for all users to access.

You can also use this setting to help you locate where your template files are located.

8. Press **Apply** and **OK**.

9. Select the **QNEW** tool button.

10.

1 Drawing1.dwg
✔ 2 Drawing2.dwg

Under Window, you see that you have two files open now. A check mark appears next to the active file.

11. Command: units

Type **units** on the command line.

12.

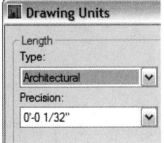

**Drawing Units**

Length
Type:
Architectural
Precision:
0'-0 1/32"

Note that the units are in Architectural.

13. Close the drawing without saving.

*Exercise 1-2:*
# Creating a New Drawing with an AEC Template

Drawing Name: New
Estimated Time: 15 minutes

This exercise reinforces the following skills:

❑ Use of templates
❑ Starting a New Drawing

| Menu | File Edit<br>New... |
|---|---|
| Toolbar | |
| Command Line | Command: new |
| Shortcut Key | Ctl + N |

1. 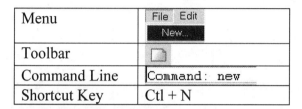 Go to **File→New**.

2.  Browse to the *Template* folder.

This should be listed under *Documents & Settings\[user name]\Local Settings\Application Data\Autodesk\ADT 2008\enu...*

3. 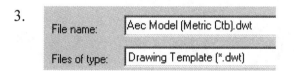 Select the Aec Model (Metric Ctb).dwt.

4. Command: units   Type **units** on the command line.

5. 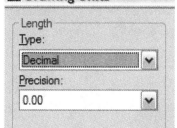 Note the units are set to Decimal.

Press **OK** to close the dialog box.

6.   Close the drawing without saving.

**TIP:**   Templates can be used to preset layers, property set definitions, dimension styles, units, and layouts.

## Setting AEC Drawing Options

| Menu | Tools→Options |
|------|---------------|
| Command line | Options |
| Context Menu→Options | Place Mouse in the graphics area and right click |
| Shortcut | Place mouse in the command line and right click |

Access the Options dialog box.

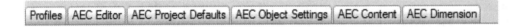

AUTOCAD ARCHITECTURE's Options includes five additional AEC specific tabs. They are AEC Editor, AEC Content, AEC Object Settings, AEC Dimension, and AEC Project Defaults.

## *AEC Editor*

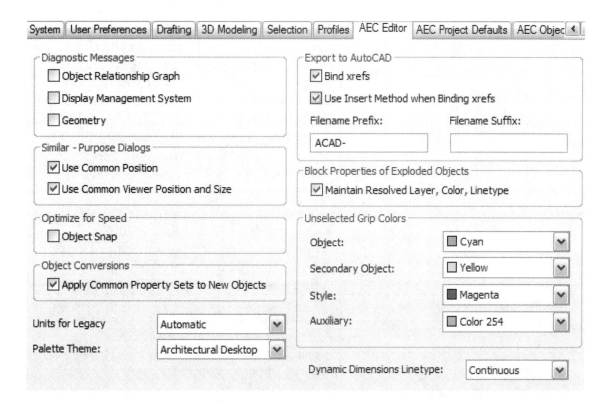

| Diagnostic Messages | All diagnostic messages are turned off by default. |
|---|---|
| **Similar-Purpose Dialogs** | Options for the position of dialog boxes and viewers. |
| **Use Common Position** | Sets one common position on the screen for similar dialog boxes, such as door, wall, and window add or modify dialog boxes. Some dialog boxes, such as those for styles and properties, are always displayed in the center of the screen, regardless of this setting. |
| **Use Common Viewer Position and Sizes** | Sets one size and position on the screen for the similar-purpose viewers in AutoCAD Architecture. Viewer position is separately controlled for add, modify, style, and properties dialog boxes. |
| **Optimize for Speed** | Options for display representations and layer loading in the Layer Manager dialog. |
| **Object Snap** | Enable to limit certain display representations to respond only to the Node and Insert object snaps. This setting affects stair, railing, space boundary, multi-view block, masking block, slice, and clip volume result (building section) objects. |

| Apply Common Property Sets to New Objects | Property sets are used for the creation of schedule tables. Each AEC object has embedded property sets, such as width and height, to be used in its schedule. AEC properties are similar to attributes. Size is a common property across most AEC objects. Occasionally, you may use a tool on an existing object and the result may be that you replace the existing object with an entirely different object. For example, if you apply the tool properties of a door to an existing window, a new door object will replace the existing window. When enabled, any property sets that were assigned to the existing window will automatically be preserved and applied to the new door provided that the property set definitions make sense. |
|---|---|
| Units for Legacy Drawings | Determines the units to be used when opening an AutoCAD drawing in AutoCAD Architecture. Automatic – uses the current AutoCAD Architecture units setting Imperial – uses Imperial units Metric – uses Metric units |
| Palette Theme | Controls the colors of Tool Palettes; you may select either AutoCAD Architecture or Windows |
| Export to AutoCAD | Enable Bind Xrefs ✻<br><br>If you enable this option, the xref will be inserted as a block and not an xref.<br><br>Enable Use Insert Method when binding Xrefs if you want all objects from an xref drawing referenced in the file you export to be automatically exploded into the host drawing.<br><br>If you enable this option, the drawing names of the xref drawings are discarded when the exported drawing is created. In addition, their layers and styles are incorporated into the host drawing. For example, all exploded walls, regardless of their source (host or xref) are located on the same layer.<br><br>Disable Use Insert Method when binding Xrefs if you want to retain the xref identities, such as layer names, when you export a file to AutoCAD or to a DXF file. For example, the blocks that define walls in the host drawing are located on A-Wall in the exploded drawing. Walls in an attached xref |

| | |
|---|---|
| | drawing are located on a layer whose name is created from the drawing name and the layer name, such as Drawing1\|WallA.<br><br>Many architects automatically bind and explode their xrefs when sending drawings to customers to protect their intellectual property.<br><br>Enter a prefix or a suffix to be added to the drawing filename when the drawing is exported to an AutoCAD drawing or a DXF file.<br><br>In order for any of these options to apply, you have to use the Export to AutoCAD command. This is available under the Files menu. |
| **Unselected Grip Colors** | Assign the colors for each type of grip |
| **Dynamic Dimensions Linetype** | Set the linetype to be used when creating dynamic dimensions. This makes it easier to distinguish between dynamic and applied dimensions. You may select either continuous or dot linetypes. |

**TIP:** Option Settings are applied to your current drawing and saved as the default settings for new drawings. Because AutoCAD Architecture operates in a Multiple Document Interface, each drawing stores the Options Settings used when it was created and last saved. Some users get confused because they open an existing drawing and it will not behave according to the current Options Settings.

## *AEC Project Defaults*

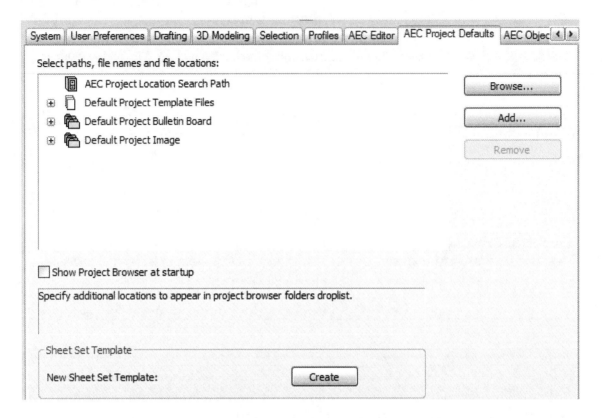

Most BID/AEC firms work in a team environment where they divide a project's tasks among several different users. The AEC Project Defaults allow the CAD Manager or team leader to select a folder on the company's server to locate files, set up template files with the project's title blocks, and even set up a webpage to post project information.

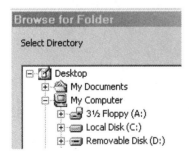

To add a path, simply expand the folder and use the Browse button to locate the desired folder.

You can add more than one path to the AEC Project Location Search Path. All the other folders only allow you to have a single location for template files, the project bulletin board, and the default project image.

**TIP:** I highly recommend that you store any custom content in a separate directory as far away from AutoCAD Architecture as possible. This will allow you to back up your custom work easily and prevent accidental erasure if you upgrade your software application.

You should be aware that AutoCAD Architecture currently allows the user to specify only ONE path for custom content, so drawings with custom commands will only work if they reside in the specified path.

☐ Show Project Browser at startup

If you enable the Show Project Browser at startup, you will automatically have access to the Project Browser whenever you start AutoCAD Architecture.

## *AEC Object Settings*

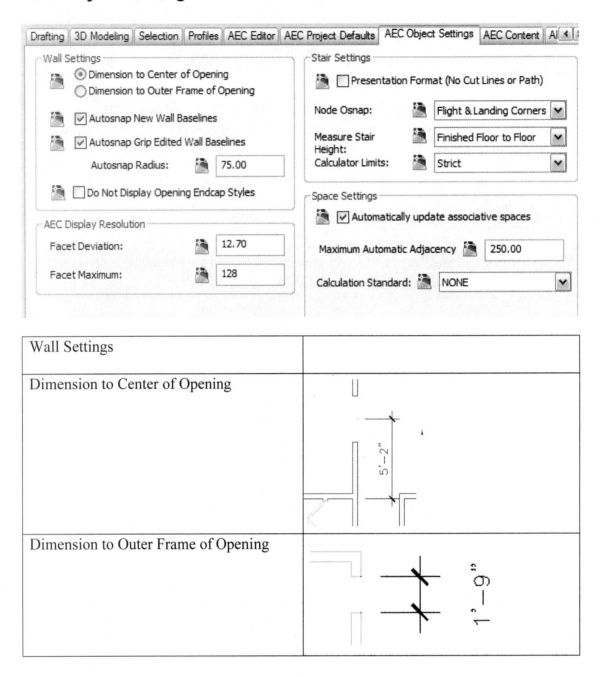

| Wall Settings | |
|---|---|
| Dimension to Center of Opening | |
| Dimension to Outer Frame of Opening | |

| | |
|---|---|
| Autosnap New Wall Baselines | Enable Autosnap New Wall Baselines to have the endpoint of a new wall that is drawn within the Autosnap Radius of the baseline of an existing wall automatically snap to that baseline.<br><br>If you select this option and set your Autosnap Radius to 0, then only walls that touch, clean up with each other. |
| Autosnap Grip Edited Wall Baselines | Enable Autosnap Grip Edited Wall Baselines to snap the endpoint of a wall that you grip edit within the Autosnap Radius of the baseline of an existing wall.<br><br>If you select this option and set your Autosnap Radius to 0, then only walls that touch clean up with each other. |
| Autosnap Radius | Enter a value to set the snap tolerance |
| Do not display opening end cap styles | Enable Do Not Display Opening Endcap Styles to suppress the display of endcaps applied to openings in walls.<br><br>Enabling this option boosts drawing performance when the drawing contains many complex endcaps. |
| Stair Settings | |
| Presentation Format (No Cut Lines or Path) | If this is enabled, a jagged line and directional arrows will not display |
| Node Osnap | Determines which snap is enabled when creating stairs:<br><br>Vertical Alignment<br>Flight and Landing Corners |
| Measure Stair Height | Rough floor to floor – ignore offsets<br>Finished floor to floor – include top and bottom offsets |

| | |
|---|---|
| Calculator Limits | Strict – stair will display a defect symbol when an edit results in a violation of the Calculation rules. Relaxed – no defect symbol will be displayed when the stair violates the Calculation rules<br><br>The Calculation rules determine how many treads are required based on the riser height and the overall height of the stairs. |
| AEC Display Resolution | This determines the resolution of arcs and circular elements.<br><br>Facet Deviation – The default is ½″<br>Facet Maximum – this can be set from 100 to 10,000.<br><br>Higher settings use more memory and may affect screen refresh rates |
| Space Settings<br><br>☑ Automatically update associative spaces<br><br>Calculation Standard:  NONE<br>NONE<br>Basic Standard<br>BOMA Standard<br>DIN Standard | If Automatically update associative spaces is enabled, AutoCAD Architecture will automatically determine which spaces are adjacent to each other and update their association accordingly.<br><br>The Maximum Automatic Adjacency sets the gap allowance between spaces for spaces to be considered adjacent.<br><br>The Floor Boundary Thickness sets the value of the Floor Boundary Thickness.<br><br>The Calculation Standard determines how the space values are calculated. |

## AEC Content

AEC DesignCenter Content Path:

| c: | Browse... |

☑ Display Edit Property Data Dialog During Tag Insertion

Tool Catalog Content Root Path:

| C:\Documents and Settings\All Users\Application Data\Autodesk\AE | Browse... |

Detail Component Databases:    Add/Remove...

Keynote Databases:    Add/Remove...

| AEC DesignCenter Content Path | Type the path and location of your content files, or click Browse to search for the content files. |
|---|---|
| Display Edit Schedule Data Dialog During Tag Insertion | To attach schedule data to objects when you insert a schedule tag in the drawing; this should be ENABLED. |
| Tool Catalog Content Root Path | Type the path and location of your Tool Catalog files, or click Browse to search for the content files. |
| Detail Component Databases | Select the **Add/Remove** button to set the search paths for your detail component files. |
| Keynote Databases | Select the **Add/Remove** button to set the search paths for your keynote database files. |

## Using AEC Content

AutoCAD Architecture uses several pre-defined and user-customizable content including:

- ❑ Architectural Display Configurations
- ❑ Architectural Profiles of Geometric Shapes
- ❑ Wall Styles and Endcap geometry
- ❑ Door styles
- ❑ Window styles
- ❑ Stair styles
- ❑ Space styles
- ❑ Schedule tables

Standard style content is stored in the AEC templates subdirectory. You can create additional content, and import or export styles between drawings.

## *AEC Dimension*

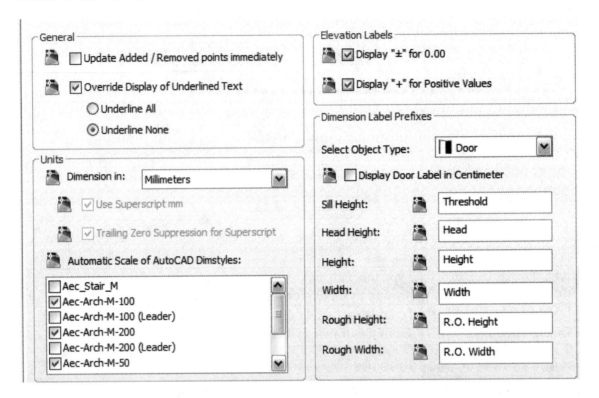

| General | |
|---|---|
| Update Added/Removed points immediately | Enable to update the display every time you add or remove a point from a dimension chain |
| Override Display of Undefined Text | Enable to automatically underline each manually overridden dimension value |
| Undefine All | Enable to manually underline overriden dimension values |
| Undefine None | Enable to not underline any overriden dimension value |
| **Units** | |
| Dimension in: | Select the desired units from the drop-down list |
| Use Superscript mm | If your units are set to meters or centimeters, enable superscripted text to display the millimeters as superscript. |

| Trailing Zero Suppression for Superscript | To suppress zeros at the end of superscripted numbers, select Trailing Zeros Suppression for Superscript.<br><br>You can select this option only if you have selected Use Superscript mm and your units are metric.<br><br>$4.12^3$ |
|---|---|
| Automatic Scale of AutoCAD Dimstyles | Select the dimstyles you would like to automatically scale when units are reset. |
| **Elevation Labels** | Select the unit in which elevation labels are to be displayed.<br><br>This unit can differ from the drawing unit. |
| Display +/- for 0.00 Values | |
| Display + for Positive Values | |
| **Dimension Label Prefixes**<br><br>Dimension Label Prefixes are set based on the object selected from the drop-down. You can set label prefixes for Doors, Windows, Openings, and Stairs.<br>Select the object, and then set the prefix for each designation. The designations will change based on the object selected. | Select Object Type:  Door<br><br>Door<br>Window<br>Opening<br>Stair<br><br>Display Door Lab<br><br>Sill Height: |

## *Accessing the Project Browser*

| Command line | AECProjectBrowser |
|---|---|
| Navigation Toolbar | ▤ |
| Files Menu | Project Browser |
| Shortcut Key | Ctl+5 |

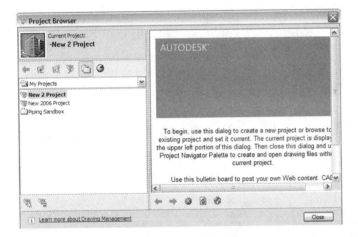

The Project Browser allows you to manage your project, similar to the old Today window in 2002, but more powerful. Projects have two parts: the building model and the reports generated from the building model. The building model is made of two drawing types: constructs and elements. A construct is any unique portion of a building. It can be a flight of stairs, a specific room, or an entire floor. Constructs are assigned to a level (floor) and a division within a project. Elements are any AEC object or content that is used multiple times in a model. For example, furniture layouts or lavatory layouts. Elements can be converted into constructs if you decide that they will not be used repeatedly.

The text you see in the right window is actually an html file. The path to this file is controlled in the path for the Default Project Bulletin Board.

| | |
|---|---|
| ✳ | New Project – creates a new project |
| ✳ | Refresh Project – updates a project |
| ✳ | Project File Navigator |

## *Architectural Profiles of Geometric Shapes*

You can create mass elements to define the shape and configuration of your preliminary study, or mass model. After you create the mass elements you need, you can change their size as necessary to reflect the building design.

- **Mass element**: A single object that has behaviors based on its shape. For example, you can set the width, depth, and height of a box mass element, and the radius and height of a cylinder mass element.

Mass elements are parametric, which allows each of the shapes to have very specific behavior when it comes to the manipulation of each mass element's shape. For example, if the corner grip point of a box is selected and dragged, then the width and depth are modified. It is easy to change the shape to another form by right-clicking on the element and selecting a new shape from the list.

Through Boolean operations (addition, subtraction, intersection), mass elements can be combined into a mass group. The mass group provides a representation of your building during the concept phase of your project.

- **Mass group**: Takes the shape of the mass elements and is placed on a separate layer from the mass elements.
- **Mass model**: A virtual mass object, shaped from mass elements, that defines the basic structure and proportion of your building. A marker appears as a small box in your drawing to which you attach mass elements.

As you continue developing your mass model, you can combine mass elements into mass groups and create complex building shapes through addition, subtraction, or intersection of mass elements. You can still edit individual mass elements attached to a mass group to further refine the building model.

To study alternative design schemes, you can create a number of mass element references. When you change the original of the referenced mass element, all the instances of the mass element references are updated.

The mass model that you create with mass elements and mass groups is a refinement of your original idea that you carry forward into the next phase of the project, in which you change the mass study into floor plates and then into walls. The walls are used to start the design phase.

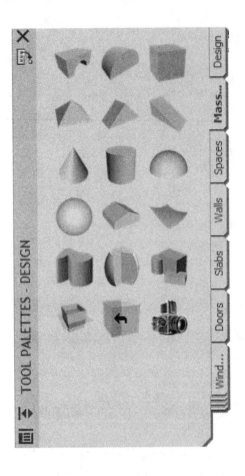

Mass Elements are accessed from the Massing Tool Palette.

To bring up the Tool Palette, press Ctl+3 and select the Massing tab.

Mass Elements that can be defined include Arches, Gables, Doric Columns, etc.

To create or add a mass element you can simply select it from the Tool Palette or type **MassElementAdd** on the command line.

## The Style Manager

| Menu | Format →Style Manager |
|---|---|
| Command Line | AecStyleManager |

The Style Manager is a Microsoft® Windows Explorer-based utility that provides you with a central location in Autodesk AutoCAD Architecture where you can view and work with styles in drawings or from Internet and intranet sites.

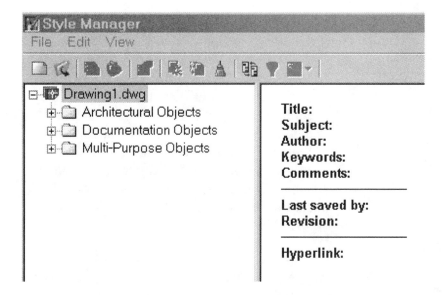

Styles are sets of parameters that you can assign to objects in Autodesk AutoCAD Architecture to determine their appearance or function. For example, a door style in Autodesk AutoCAD Architecture determines what door type, such as single or double, bi-fold or hinged, a door in a drawing represents. You can assign one style to more than one object, and you can modify the style to change the all the objects that are assigned that style.

Depending on your design projects, either you or your CAD Manager might want to customize existing styles or create new styles. The Style Manager allows you to easily create, customize, and share styles with other users. With the Style Manager, you can:

- Provide a central point for accessing styles from open drawings and Internet and intranet sites

- Quickly set up new drawings and templates by copying styles from other drawings or templates

- Sort and view the styles in your drawings and templates by drawing or by style type

- Preview an object with a selected style

- Create new styles and edit existing styles

- Delete unused styles from drawings and templates

- Send styles to other Autodesk AutoCAD Architecture users by email

Objects in Autodesk AutoCAD Architecture that use styles include 2D sections and elevations, AEC Polygons, curtain walls, curtain wall units, doors, endcaps, railings, roof slab edges, roof slabs, schedule tables, slab edges, slabs, spaces, stairs, structural members, wall modifiers, walls, window assemblies, and windows.

Additionally, layer key styles, schedule data formats, and cleanup group, mask block, multi-view block, profile, and property set definitions are handled by the Style Manager.

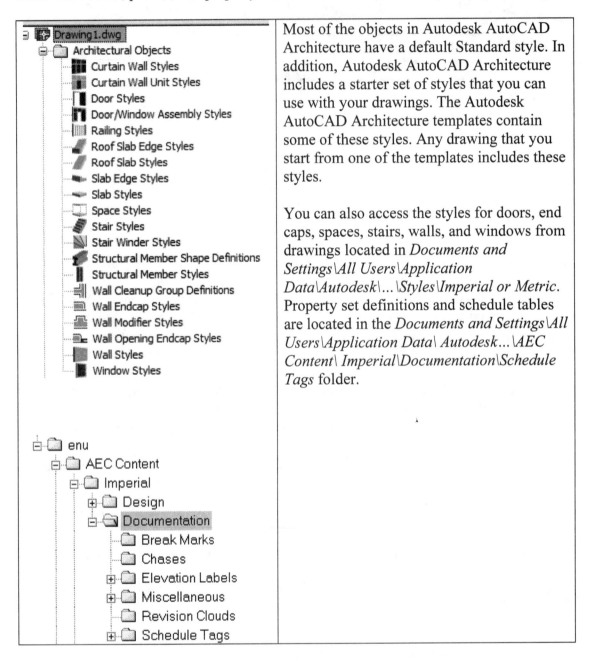

Most of the objects in Autodesk AutoCAD Architecture have a default Standard style. In addition, Autodesk AutoCAD Architecture includes a starter set of styles that you can use with your drawings. The Autodesk AutoCAD Architecture templates contain some of these styles. Any drawing that you start from one of the templates includes these styles.

You can also access the styles for doors, end caps, spaces, stairs, walls, and windows from drawings located in *Documents and Settings\All Users\Application Data\Autodesk\...\Styles\Imperial or Metric*. Property set definitions and schedule tables are located in the *Documents and Settings\All Users\Application Data\ Autodesk...\AEC Content\ Imperial\Documentation\Schedule Tags* folder.

**TIP:** I do not recommend modifying AutoCAD Architecture's standard styles as this may affect drawings you bring in from outside sources. Instead, copy the existing style to a NEW style and modify it using the desired properties.

*Exercise 1-3:*
## Creating a New Geometric Profile

Drawing Name:      New using Imperial.dwt
Estimated Time:    15 minutes

This exercise reinforces the following skills:

- ❑ Use of AEC Design Content
- ❑ Use of Mass Elements

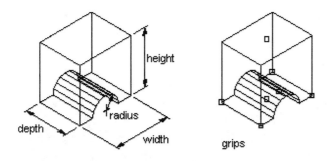

*Creating an arch mass element*

1.  Start a New Drawing.

    Select the QNEW tool from the Standard toolbar.

    Because we assigned a template in Exercise 1-2, a drawing file opens without prompting us to select a template.

2.  Select the **Tool Palettes** tool from the Standard toolbar if the Tool Palette is not visible.

3.      Select the Massing tab on the Tool Palette.

    Select the Arch icon.

4.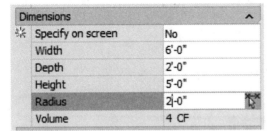

Expand the Dimensions section.

Set Specify on screen to No.
Set the Width to 6'-0".
Set the Depth to 2'-0".
Set the Height to 5'-0".
Set the Radius to 2'-0".

5.

Pick a point any where in the drawing area.

Press ENTER to accept a Rotation Angle of 0 or right click and select ENTER.

Press ENTER to exit the command.

6. Switch to an isometric view.

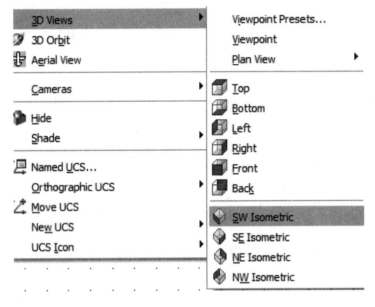

If you are unable to locate the View toolbar, simply go to **View→3D Views→SW Isometric**.

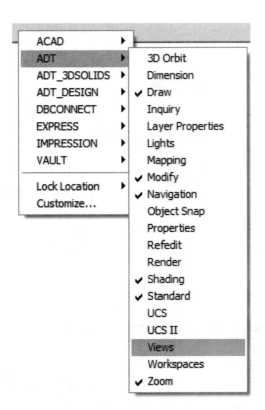

To bring up the Views toolbar so it is always available to you:

Right click on any toolbar.
Go to **ADT** and left click on **Views**.

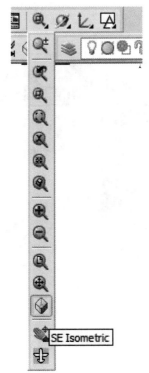

The Zoom flyout on the Navigation toolbar includes an SE Isometric tool to allow you to quickly switch to an isometric view.

The Zoom toolbar also has an Isometric View tool included.

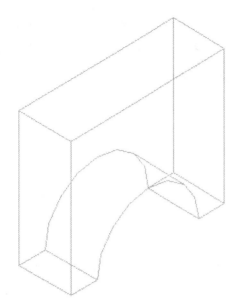

7.  Select the **Realistic** tool from the Shading toolbar.

You can also type **SHA** on the command line, then **R** for Realistic.

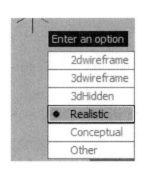

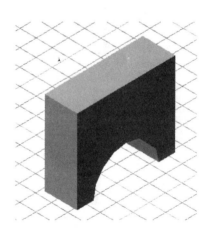

8. To change the arch properties, select the arch so that it is highlighted. Right click and select 'Properties.'

9. 

| Dimensions | |
| --- | --- |
| Width | 6'-0" |
| Depth | 2'-0" |
| Height | 5'-0" |
| Radius | 2'-6" |
| Volume | 41 CF |

Change the Radius to 2'-6".

Pick into the graphics window and the arch will update.

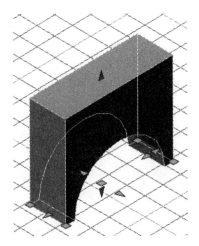

Press ESC to release the grips on the arc.

10.  Save the drawing as ex1-3.dwg.

**Exercise 1-4:**
## Creating a New Visual Style

Drawing Name:     ex1-3.dwg
Estimated Time:     30 minutes

This exercise reinforces the following skills:

- ❑  Use of Visual Styles
- ❑  Controlling the Display of Objects

1.     Open *ex1-3.dwg*.

2.     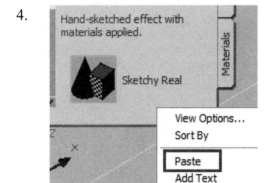 Left click on the title bar for the Tool Palette.

Left click on **Visualization**.

3.     Highlight the **Conceptual** tool.

Right click and select **Copy**.

4.     Scroll to the bottom of the palette.

Right click and select **Paste**.

5.     Highlight the copied tool.
Right click and select **Rename**.

6.  Change the name to **Real Conceptual**.

7. 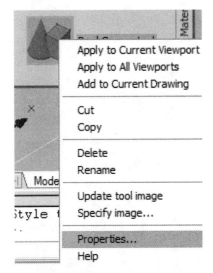 Highlight, right click and select **Properties**.

8. 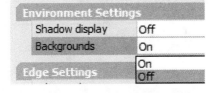 Under Materials and Color:

Set Materials to **Materials and textures**.

9. 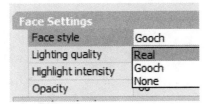 Under Environment Settings:

Set the Backgrounds to **Off**.

10. 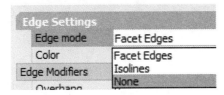 Under Face Settings:

Set the Face Style to **Real**.

11. Under Edge Settings:

Set the Edge mode to **None**.

12. Press **OK** to close the Properties dialog.

13. Save the drawing as *ex1-4.dwg*.

**TIP:** If you aren't sure what a setting does, look at the bottom of the dialog. When a field is selected, a small help message appears.

> Sets edge display to Facet, Isolines, or None. (VSEDGES system variable)

*Exercise 1-5:*
## Creating a New Wall Style

Drawing Name:     New using Imperial.dwt
Estimated Time:     30 minutes

This exercise reinforces the following skills:

❑   Use of AEC Design Content
❑   Use of Wall Styles

1.   Start a New Drawing.

Select the QNEW tool from the Standard toolbar.

2.   Type Ctl+3 to activate the Tool Palette if it is not currently visible.

3.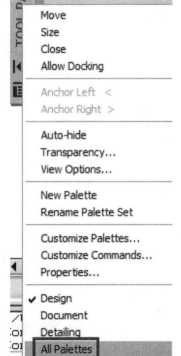

Right click on the Tool Palettes bar.

Enable **All Palettes**.

4.

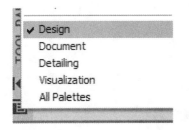

Right click on the Palette tabs to see a list of all the palettes available.

Right click on the Tool Palette title bar.

Select **Design** to make the Design Tool Palette active.

Select the **Walls** tab.

5.

Highlight the first wall icon.

Right click and select **Wall Styles**.

6.  The Style Manager is displayed, with the current drawing expanded in the tree view. The wall styles in the current drawing are displayed under the wall style type. All other style and definition types are filtered out in the tree view.

    Select the **New Style** tool.

7.  Change the name of the new style by typing 'Brick_Block.'

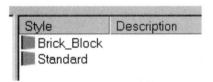

8.  The Wall Style Properties dialog appears.

9.

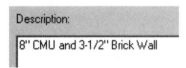

    In the General tab, type in the description **8″ CMU and 3-1/2″ Brick Wall** in the Description field as shown.

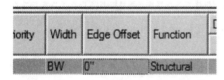

## Adding Wall Components

10. Select the Components tab.
    Change the Name to **CMU** by typing in the Name field indicated.
    Press the dropdown arrow next to the Edge Offset Button.
    Set the Edge Offset to 0″.

| iority | Width | Edge Offset | Function |
|--------|-------|-------------|----------|
|        | BW    | 0″          | Structural |

    A 0″ edge offset specifies that the outside edge of the CMU is coincident with the wall baseline.

11. Press the Width down arrow button.

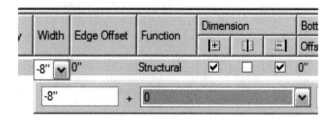

Set the value to -8″.

This specifies that the CMU has a fixed width of 8″ in the negative direction from the wall baseline (to the inside).

12. You now have one component defined for your wall named CMU with the properties shown.

Next, we'll add wall insulation.

 Press the Add Component button on the right side of the dialog box.

13. In the Name field, type **Insulation**.

Set the Priority to 1. (The lower the priority number, the higher the priority when creating intersections.)

Set the Edge Offset with a value of **0″**.

Set the Component Width as shown, with a value of 1.5″ and the Base Width set to 0.

This specifies that the insulation has a fixed width of 1.5″ offset in a positive direction from the wall baseline (to the outside).

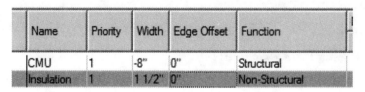

| Name | Priority | Width | Edge Offset | Function |
|------|----------|-------|-------------|----------|
| CMU | 1 | -8″ | 0″ | Structural |
| Insulation | 1 | 1 1/2″ | 0″ | Non-Structural |

14.
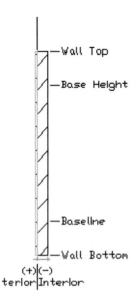

Note that the preview changes to show the insulation component.

15. Now, we add an air space component to our wall.

 Press the Add Component button.

16. Rename the new component **Air Space**.

Set the Edge Offset to **0″**.

This specifies that the inside edge of the air space is coincident with the outside edge of the insulation.

The width should be set to **1″**.

This specifies that the air gap will have a fixed width of 1″ offset in the positive direction from the wall baseline (to the outside).

| Name | Priority | Width | Edge Offset | Function |
|------|----------|-------|-------------|----------|
| CMU | 1 | -8″ | 0″ | Structural |
| Insulation | 1 | 1 1/2″ | 0″ | Non-Structural |
| Air Space | 1 | 1″ | 0″ | Non-Structural |

17. Use the **Add Component** tool to add the fourth component.

The Name should be **Brick**.
The Priority set to **1**.
The Edge Offset set to **2.5″**.
The Width set to **3.5″**.

The Function should be set to **Structural**.

| Name | Priority | Width | Edge Offset | Function |
|------|----------|-------|-------------|----------|
| CMU | 1 | -8″ | 0″ | Structural |
| Insulation | 1 | 1 1/2″ | 0″ | Non-Structural |
| Air Space | 1 | 1″ | 0″ | Non-Structural |
| Brick | 1 | 3 1/2″ | 2 1/2″ | Structural |

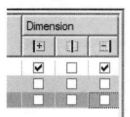

The Dimension section allows you to define where the extension lines for your dimension will be placed when measuring the wall. In this case, we are not interested in including the air space or insulation in our linear dimensions.

18.

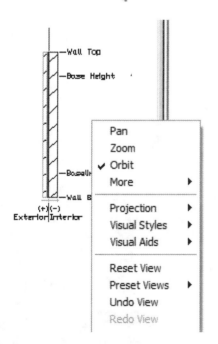

Note how your wall style previews.

If you right click in the preview pane, you can change the preview window by zooming, panning, or assigning a Preset View.

The preview pane uses a DWF-style interface.

## Assigning Materials

19. Select the Materials tab.

Highlight the **CMU** component.

 Select the **Add New Material** tool.

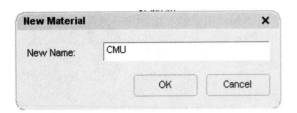

20. Enter **CMU** in the New Name field and press **OK**.

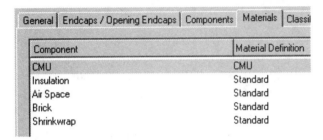

21. Use the **Add New Material** tool to assign new materials to each component.

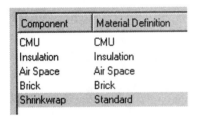

## Defining Display Properties

22. Highlight the **CMU** Component.

 Select the **Edit Material** tool.

Select the **Display Properties** tab.

Highlight the **General** Display Representation.

Click on the **Style Override** button.

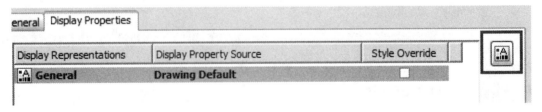

23.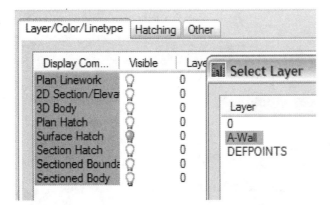

Select the **Layer/Color/ Linetype** tab.

Highlight all the components. Press the Layer column.

Set the Layer to **A-Wall**.

24.

Select the **Hatching** tab.

Highlight **Plan Hatch** and select **Pattern**.

Under Type, select **Predefined**.

Under Pattern Name, select **AR-B88**.

25. Assign the **AR-B88** Pattern to all the Display Components.

Set the Angles to **0**.

Press **OK** twice to return to the Materials tab of the Wall Properties dialog.

26.   Highlight **Insulation** and select the **Edit Material** tool.

Select the **Display Properties** tab.

Highlight the **General** Display Property.

Click on the **Style Override** button.

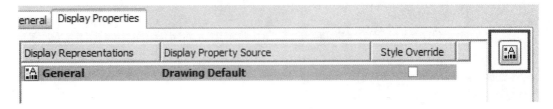

27. Select the **Hatching** tab.

Select all the Display Components so they all are highlighted.

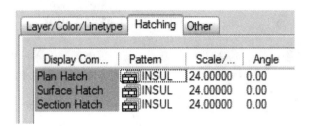 Set the Plan Hatch to the **INSUL** pattern under Predefined type.

Set the Angle to **0.00**.

28. Press **OK** twice to return to the previous dialog.

29. Highlight **Brick** and select the **Edit Material** tool.

    Select the **Display Properties** tab.

    Highlight the **General** Display Representation.

    Click on the **Style Override** button.

30. 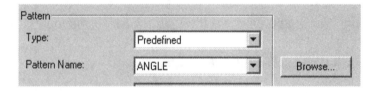 Select the **Hatching** tab.

    Highlight the three display components.

    Select the first pattern.

31. Set the Type to **Predefined**.

32. Select the **Browse** button.

    | Pattern | | |
    |---|---|---|
    | Type: | Predefined ▼ | |
    | Pattern Name: | ANGLE ▼ | Browse... |

33.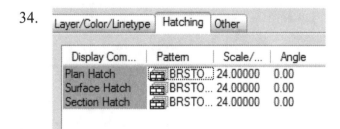

    BRSTONE    Select the **BRSTONE** pattern.

34. Set the Angle to 0 for all hatches.

    Press **OK** twice.

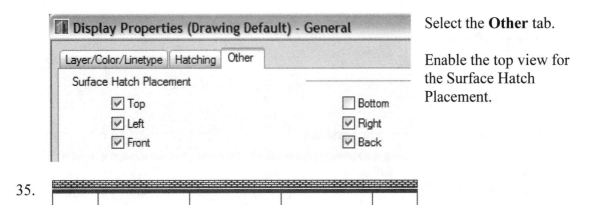

Select the **Other** tab.

Enable the top view for the Surface Hatch Placement.

35.

Press OK to exit the Edit dialog.
You can preview how the changes you made to the material display will appear when you create your wall.

Close the Style Manager.

36.   Save as *ex1-5.dwg*.

*Exercise 1-6:*
## Creating a Tool

Drawing Name:    ex1-6.dwg
Estimated Time:    30 minutes

This exercise reinforces the following skills:

- ❑ Use of AEC Design Content
- ❑ Use of Wall Styles

1. Open or continue working in *ex1-5.dwg*.

2.     Go to **Format→Style Manager** to launch the Style Manager.

    Format  Window  Help
       Style Manager...
       Display Manager...

3.     Wall Styles
         Brick_Block
         Standard
        Locate the Brick-Block wall style you created.

4.     Drag and drop the wall style onto your Walls Palette.

    Brick_Block     Press OK to close the Style Manager.

5.     Highlight the tool.
    Right click and select **Rename**.

    Apply Tool Properties to
    Re-import 'Brick_Block' Wall Style
    Wall Styles...

    Cut
    Copy

    Delete
    Rename

6. 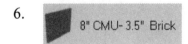 Change the name to **8″ CMU- 3.5″ Brick**.

7.

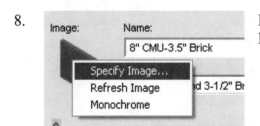

Highlight **8″ CMU- 3.5″ Brick** tool.

Right click and select **Properties**.

8.

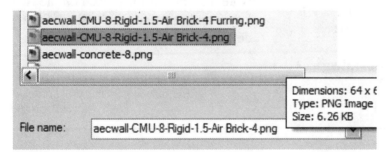

Highlight the image icon in the dialog.
Right click and select **Specify Image**.

9. Locate the file called **aecwall-CMU-8-Rigid-1.5 Air Brick-4.png**.

Press **Open**.

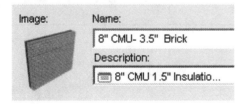

The image is reset.

Press **OK**.

## Organizing your Palette

10.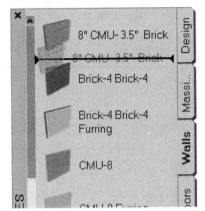
Drag the new tool to the top of your palette.

11. Select the new tool and draw a wall.
You may draw a wall simply by picking two points.

    If you enable the ORTHO button on the bottom of the screen, your wall will be straight.

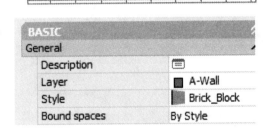

12.

Select the wall you drew.

Right click and select **Properties**.

Note that the wall is placed on the A-Wall Layer and uses the Brick-Block Style you defined.

13. Save your file as **Styles1.dwg**.

---

**TIP:** The wall style you created will not be available in any new drawings unless you copy it over to the default template.

---

*Exercise 1-7:*
## Copying a Style to a Template

Drawing Name:     Styles1.dwg
Estimated Time:   20 minutes

This exercise reinforces the following skills:

- Use of Styles
- Use of Templates

1.  Open *Styles1.dwg*.
    You can also open any drawing that contains the styles you wish to add to your template.

2.  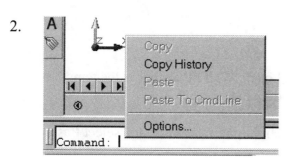     Place your cursor in your command line.

    Right click on your mouse.

    A short cut menu will appear.

    Select **Options**.

3.

    Select the **Files** tab.
    Browse down to the Drawing Template Settings section.
    Expand this section and determine the file you have set as the Default Template File Name for **QNEW**.

    This is the file that is used as a template every time you select the **QNEW** button.

4.  Open the file you have specified as your default template.

5.  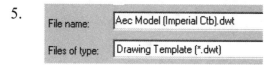     You need to set the Files of type to Drawing Template in order to see the file.

6. 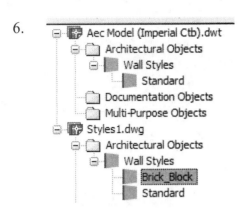 Locate the **Brick_Block** Wall Style in the *Styles1.dwg*.

7. Right click and select **Copy**.

8. 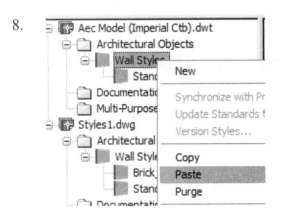 Locate Wall Styles under the template drawing.

Highlight, right click and select **Paste**.

9. Close the Style Manager.

10. Save and close the template drawing file.

11. Select the **QNEW** tool.

12. Enable the Design Tool Palette.

13. Select the **Walls** tab.

14.  Highlight a Wall tool on the Tool Palette.

Right click and select **Wall Styles**.

15.  You see that the *Brick-Block* wall style is available in the current drawing.

Close the *Styles* dialog.

16. Close all drawing files without saving.

---

**TIP:** A fast way to close all open files is to type **CLOSEALL** on the command line. You will be prompted to save any unsaved files.

---

### Exercise 1-8:
## Downloading Styles from Autodesk's Website

Drawing Name:     Styles1.dwg
Estimated Time:     15 minutes

This exercise reinforces the following skills:

- ❑  Use of AEC Design Content
- ❑  Use of Wall Styles

> **NOTE:    This exercise requires access to the Internet.**
> **idrop capability should also have been installed.**

1.    Open the *Styles1.dwg*.

2.    Select the **Design Center** tool from the Standard toolbar.

     You can also press **Ctl+2** on your keyboard.

3.    Select the **DC Online** tab.
      Scroll down to the 3D Architectural heading.
      Select the + symbol to expand the folder.

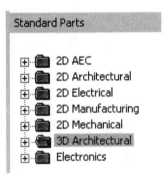

4.        Browse to the *Windows* folder under *3D Architectural/ Doors and Windows/.*

5.    Click on a window.

     Your cursor changes to an idrop.

In order to access idrop capabilities, you need to download the idrop software. This is available for free from Autodesk's website.

You will know idrop is properly installed, if you see an eyedropper when you mouse over an idrop-enabled object.

6.    Place your cursor next to the wall you drew in the previous exercise.

7.  Pick to place the window into the wall.

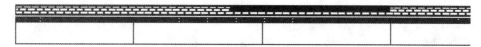

8.  If you mouse over the window, a hyperlink is displayed.

9.  Close the Design Center.

10. Save the file as *Styles2.dwg*.

## Layer Manager

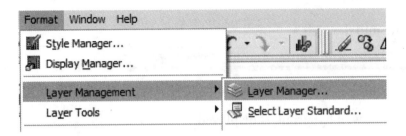

Back in the days of vellum and pencil, drafters would use separate sheets to organize their drawings, so one sheet might have the floor plan, one sheet the site plan, etc. The layers of paper would be placed on top of each other and the transparent quality of the vellum would allow the drafter to see the details on the lower sheets. Different colored pencils would be used to make it easier for the drafter to locate and identify elements of a drawing, such as dimensions, electrical outlets, water lines, etc.

When drafting moved to Computer Aided Design, the concept of sheets was transferred to the use of Layers. Drafters could assign a Layer Name, color, linetype, etc. and then place different elements on the appropriate layer.

AutoCAD Architecture is unique in that it has a Layer Management system to allow the user to implement AIA standards easily.

## Layer Manager

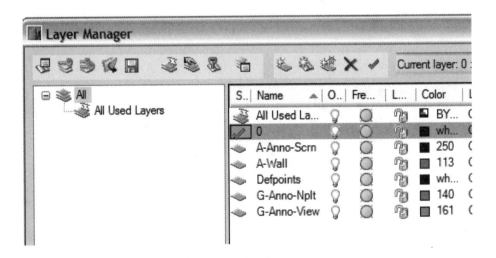

The Layer Manager helps you organize, sort, and group layers, as well as save and coordinate layering schemes. You can also use layering standards with the Layer Manager to better organize the layers in your drawings.

When you open the Layer Manager, all the layers in the current drawing are displayed in the right panel. You can work with individual layers to:

- Change layer properties by selecting the property icons
- Make a layer the current layer
- Create, rename, and delete layers

If you are working with drawings that contain large numbers of layers, you can improve the speed at which the Layer Manager loads layers when you open it by selecting the Layer Manager/Optimize for Speed option in your AEC Editor options.

The Layer Manager has a toolbar as shown.

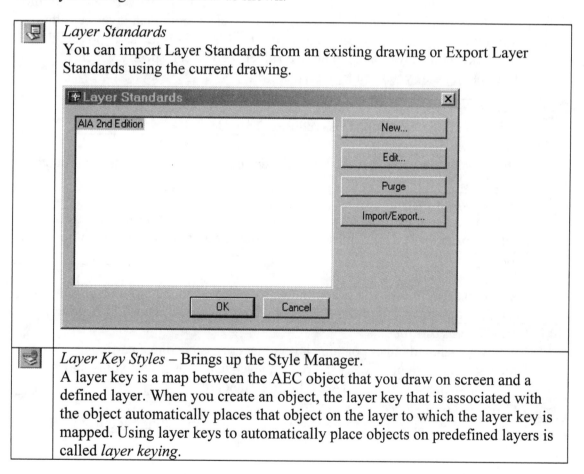

| | *Layer Standards* |
|---|---|
| | You can import Layer Standards from an existing drawing or Export Layer Standards using the current drawing. |
| | *Layer Key Styles* – Brings up the Style Manager. |
| | A layer key is a map between the AEC object that you draw on screen and a defined layer. When you create an object, the layer key that is associated with the object automatically places that object on the layer to which the layer key is mapped. Using layer keys to automatically place objects on predefined layers is called *layer keying*. |

**TIP:** The layer key styles in Autodesk AutoCAD Architecture, Release 3 and above replace the use of LY files. If you have LY files from S8 or Release 1 of AutoCAD AutoCAD Architecture that you want to use, then you can create a new layer key style from an LY file. On the command line enter **-AecLYImport** to import legacy LY files.

| | |
|---|---|
| | *Layer Key Overrides*<br>You can apply overrides to any layer keys within a layer key style that is based on a layer standard. The structure of the layer name of each layer that each layer key maps an object to is determined by the descriptive fields in the layer standard definition. You can override the information in each field according to the values set in the layer standard definition. You can allow overrides on all the layer keys within a layer key style, or you can select individual layer keys that you want to override. You can also choose to allow all of the descriptive fields that make up the layer name to be overridden, or you can specify which descriptive fields you want to override. |
| | *Load Filter Groups*<br>This tool allows you to load a saved filter group. |
| | *Save Filter Groups*<br>This tool allows you to save a defined filter group, so that you can use it in other drawings. |
| | *New Property Filter*<br>A Property Filter displays only layers that meet a certain criteria, such as color, color, frozen/thawed, or names. You can specify more than one type of property for a filter. |
| | *New Group Filter*<br>A Group Filter allows you to combine a set of layers together into a group. You can then turn on and off several layers by controlling the status of the group. |
| | *New Standards Filter*<br>A Layer Standards filter contains layers that are assigned to a particular standard. For example, you can create a layer standards filter to only show layers associated with the AIA 2$^{nd}$ Edition standard. |
| | *Layer States Manager*<br>The Layer States Manager allows you save your layer settings and restore them. |
| | *New Layer*<br>Creates a new layer. |

*New Layer from Standard*

Creates a new layer based on an existing layer standard.

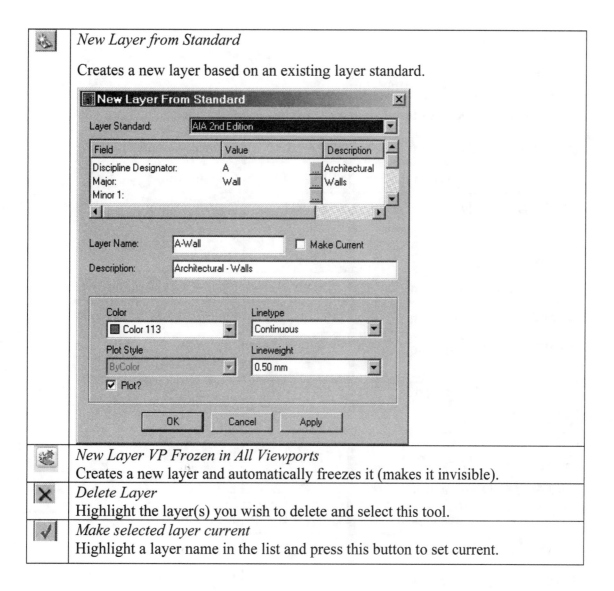

*New Layer VP Frozen in All Viewports*
Creates a new layer and automatically freezes it (makes it invisible).

*Delete Layer*
Highlight the layer(s) you wish to delete and select this tool.

*Make selected layer current*
Highlight a layer name in the list and press this button to set current.

The following are the default layer keys used by Autodesk AutoCAD Architecture when you create AEC objects.

## Default layer keys for creating AEC objects

| Layer Key | Description | Layer Key | Description |
|---|---|---|---|
| ANNDTOBJ | Detail marks | CONTROL | Control systems |
| ANNELOBJ | Elevation objects | CWLAYOUT | Curtain walls |
| ANNOBJ | Notes, leaders, etc. | CWUNIT | Curtain wall units |
| ANNREV | Revisions | DIMLINE | Dimensions |
| ANNSXKEY | Section marks | DIMMAN | Dimensions (AutoCAD points) |
| ANNSXOBJ | Section marks | DOOR | Doors |
| ANNSYMOBJ | Annotation marks | DOORNO | Door tags |
| APPL | Appliances | DRAINAGE | Drainage |
| AREA | Areas | ELEC | Electric |
| AREAGRP | Area groups | ELECNO | Electrical tags |
| AREAGRPNO | Area group tags | ELEV | Elevations |
| AREANO | Area tags | ELEVAT | Elevators |
| CAMERA | Cameras | ELEVHIDE | Elevations (2D) |
| CASE | Casework | EQUIP | Equipment |
| CASENO | Casework tags | EQUIPNO | Equipment tags |
| CEILGRID | Ceiling grids | FINCEIL | Ceiling tags |
| CEILOBJ | Ceiling objects | FINFLOOR | Finish tags |
| CHASE | Chases | FIRE | Fire system equip. |
| COLUMN | Columns | FURN | Furniture |
| COMMUN | Communication | FURNNO | Furniture tags |

| Layer Key | Description | Layer Key | Description |
|-----------|-------------|-----------|-------------|
| GRIDBUB | Plan grid bubbles | SITE | Site |
| GRIDLINE | Column grids | SLAB | Slabs |
| LAYGRID | Layout grids | SPACEBDRY | Space boundaries |
| LIGHTCLG | Ceiling lighting | SPACEOBJ | Space objects |
| LIGHTW | Wall lighting | STAIR | Stairs |
| MASSELEM | Massing elements | STAIRH | Stair handrails |
| MASSGRPS | Massing groups | STRUCTBEAM | Structural beams |
| MASSSLCE | Massing slices | STRUCTBEAMIDEN | Structural beam tags |
| OPENING | Wall openings | STRUCTBRACE | Structural braces |
| PEOPLE | People | STRUCTBRACEIDEN | Structural brace tags |
| PFIXT | Plumbing fixtures | STRUCTCOLS | Structural columns |
| PLANTS | Plants - outdoor | STRUCTCOLSIDEN | Structural column tags |
| PLANTSI | Plants - indoor | SWITCH | Electrical switches |
| POLYGON | AEC Polygons | TITTEXT | Border and title block |
| POWER | Electrical power | TOILACC | Arch. specialties |
| PRK-SYM | Parking symbols | TOILNO | Toilet tags |
| ROOF | Rooflines | UTIL | Site utilities |
| ROOFSLAB | Roof slabs | VEHICLES | Vehicles |
| ROOMNO | Room tags | WALL | Walls |
| SCHEDOBJ | Schedule tables | WALLFIRE | Fire wall patterning |
| SEATNO | Seating tags | WALLNO | Wall tags |
| SECT | Miscellaneous sections | WIND | Windows |
| SECTHIDE | Sections (2D) | WINDASSEM | Window assemblies |
|  |  | WINDNO | Window tags |

## Desktop Display Manager

| Menu | Format →Display Manager |
|---|---|
| Command Line | DisplayManager |

Exercise 1-9:
## Exploring the Display Manager

Drawing Name:     ex1-4.dwg
Estimated Time:     15 minutes

This exercise reinforces the following skills:

❑   Display Manager

1.     Open *ex1-4.dwg*.

2.     Access the Display Manager using the Menu.
       Go to **Format →Display Manager**.

3.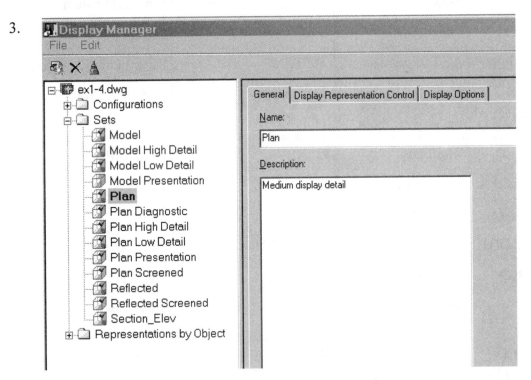

The display system in Autodesk AutoCAD Architecture controls how AEC objects
are displayed in a designated viewport. By specifying the AEC objects you want to
display in a viewport and the direction from which you want to view them, you can
produce different architectural displays, such as floor plans, reflected plans,
elevations, 3D models, or schematic displays.

4.

- Door
  - Elevation
  - Model
  - Model High Detail
  - Model Low Detail
  - Nominal
  - Plan
  - Plan High Detail
  - Plan Low Detail
  - Plan Screened
  - Reflected
  - Reflected Screened
  - Threshold Plan
  - Threshold Plan Screened
  - Threshold Symbol Plan

Expand the *Representations by Object* folder.

Locate Door.

You see that there are different ways a door will appear depending on the display configuration selected.

Highlight **Threshold Plan**.

5.

| Display Component | Visible |
|---|---|
| Threshold A | |
| Threshold B | |
| Threshold A Above Cut Plane | |
| Threshold B Above Cut Plane | |
| Threshold A Below Cut Plane | |
| Threshold B Below Cut Plane | |

You see that the Threshold visibilities are turned off.

6.

| Display Component | Visible |
|---|---|
| Door Panel | |
| Frame | |
| Stop | |
| Swing | |
| Direction | |
| Door Panel Above Cut Plane | |
| Frame Above Cut Plane | |
| Stop Above Cut Plane | |
| Swing Above Cut Plane | |
| Door Panel Below Cut Plane | |
| Frame Below Cut Plane | |
| Stop Below Cut Plane | |
| Swing Below Cut Plane | |

Highlight the Plan configuration. You see that some door components are turned on and others are turned off.

7.

| Layer/Color/Linetype | Muntins | Other |
|---|---|---|

| Display Component | Visible |
|---|---|
| Door Panel | |
| Frame | |
| Stop | |
| Swing | |
| Glass | |

Highlight the Model configuration.

8.

⊟ 📁 Sets
　　🔳 Model
　　🔳 Model High Detail
　　🔳 Model Low Detail
　　🔳 Model Presentation
　　🔳 **Plan**

Go to the Sets folder. The Set highlighted in bold is the active Display Representation.

Highlight Plan.

9.

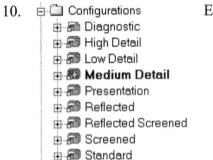

Select the Display Representation Control tab.
Locate **Door** under Objects.
Note that some display representations are checked and others are unchecked.
A check indicates that the door is visible. Which door components are visible is controlled under Representations by Object.

10.

⊟ 📁 Configurations
　　⊞ 🔲 Diagnostic
　　⊞ 🔲 High Detail
　　⊞ 🔲 Low Detail
　　⊞ 🔲 **Medium Detail**
　　⊞ 🔲 Presentation
　　⊞ 🔲 Reflected
　　⊞ 🔲 Reflected Screened
　　⊞ 🔲 Screened
　　⊞ 🔲 Standard

Expand the Configurations folder.

11.

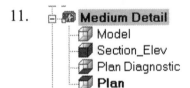

Expand Medium Detail.
You see the different display sets. Note that Medium Detail does not hold all the different display sets. You can add or remove display sets.
Close the Display Manager.

12. Close the drawing without saving.

## Lesson 2:
# Site Plans

Most architectural projects start with a site plan. The site plan indicates the property lines, the house location, a North symbol, any streets surrounding the property, topographical features, location of sewer, gas, and/or electrical lines (assuming they are below ground – above ground connections are not shown), and topographical features.

When laying out the floor plan for the house, many architects take into consideration the path of sun (to optimize natural light), street access (to locate the driveway), and any noise factors. AutoCAD Architecture includes the ability to perform sun studies on your models.

AutoCAD Architecture allows the user to simulate the natural path of the sun based on the longitude and latitude coordinates of the site, so you can test how natural light will affect various house orientations.

A plot plan must include the following features:

- Length and bearing of each property line
- Location, outline, and size of buildings on the site
- Contour of the land
- Elevation of property corners and contour lines
- North symbol
- Trees, shrubs, streams, and other topological items
- Streets, sidewalks, driveways, and patios
- Location of utilities
- Easements and drainages (if any)
- Well, septic, sewage line, and underground cables
- Fences and retaining walls
- Lot number and/or address of the site
- Scale of the drawing

The plot plan is drawn using information provided by the county/city and/or a licensed surveyor.

It used to be that you would draw to a scale, such as $1/8'' = 1'$, but with AutoCAD Architecture, you draw full-size and then set up your layout to the proper scale. This ensures that all items you draw will fit together properly.

*Exercise 2-1:*
## Installing the Express Tools

Drawing Name:     None
Estimated Time:     15 minutes

This exercise reinforces the following skills:

- ❑ Modifying the Software Installation
- ❑ Customization
- ❑ Express Tools

The Express Tools are not installed using the default installation. If you did not install the Express Tools during your first installation, you can add them later. You will need your installation CD to complete the installation.

1. Close all applications, including AutoCAD Architecture. Turn off any virus checking software, such as Norton.

2. Go to the **Control Panel→Add/Remove Software**.

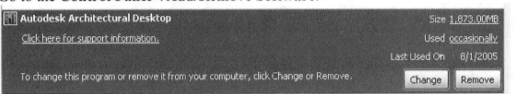

3. Locate the installation of Autodesk AutoCAD Architecture 2008. Select **Change**.

4. 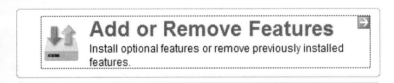     Select **Add or Remove Features**.

5.      Locate the *Express Tools* and select it to be installed on the local hard drive.

6. Press Next.

7.    **Configure Content Packs**                                    Press **Next**.

| Content Pack | Desktop Shortcut |
|---|---|
| **Autodesk Content Packs** | |
| ☑ Architectural Desktop Content - Imperial | Yes |
| ☑ Architectural Desktop Content - Metric | Yes |
| ☐ Architectural Desktop Content - Metric D A CH | Yes |

Press **Next** again to confirm the choices.

8. Press **Finish** to conclude the update.

*Exercise 2-2:*
## *Creating Custom Line Types*

Drawing Name:      New
Estimated Time:    15 minutes

This exercise reinforces the following skills:

- ❑ Creation of linetypes
- ❑ Customization

Architectural drafting requires a variety of custom linetypes in order to display specific features. The standard linetypes provided with AutoCAD Architecture are insufficient from an architectural point of view. You may find custom linetypes on Autodesk's website, www.cadalog.com, or any number of websites on the Internet. However, the ability to create linetypes as needed is an excellent skill for an architectural drafter.

It's a good idea to store any custom linetypes in a separate file. The standard file for storing linetypes is acad.lin. If you store any custom linetypes in acad.lin file, you will lose them the next time you upgrade your software.

1.

| Express | 3D Solids | Design | Wind |
| --- | --- | --- | --- |
| Blocks | ▸ |
| Text | ▸ |
| Layout tools | ▸ |
| Dimension | ▸ |
| Selection tools | ▸ |
| Modify | ▸ |
| Draw | ▸ |
| File tools | ▸ |
| Web tools | ▸ |
| Tools | ▸ |
| Web Links | ▸ |
| Express Tools FAQ | |
| Help | |

Once the Express Tools are installed, you can start this exercise.

To verify that the Express Tools are installed, simply look at your menu headings.

2.    Start a new drawing using **QNEW**.

3.    _____    _____    _____    _____

Draw a property line.
This property line was created as follows:
   Set ORTHO ON.
   Draw a horizontal line 12 units long
   Use SNAP FROM to start the next line @3,0 distance from the previous line.
   The short line is 6 units long.
   Use SNAP FROM to start the next line @3,0 distance from the previous line.
   The second short line is 6 units long.
   Use SNAP FROM to start the next line @3,0 distance from the previous line.
   Draw a second horizontal line 12 units long.

4.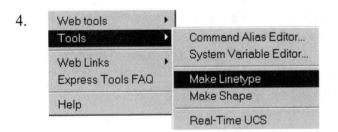

Go to **Express→Tools→Make Linetype**.

5.    Create a file name called custom-arch.lin and press 'Save.'

**TIP:** Place all your custom linetypes in a single drawing file and then use the AutoCAD Design Center to help you locate and load the desired linetype.

6. When prompted for the linetype name, type: property-line.
   When prompted for the linetype description, type: property-line
   Specify starting point for line definition; select the far left point of the line type.
   Specify ending point for line definition; select the far right point of the line type.
   When prompted to select the objects, start at the long line on the left and pick the line segments in order.

7. Go to **Format→Linetype**.

8.

| Current Linetype: ByLayer | | |
|---|---|---|
| Linetype | Appearance | Description |
| ByLayer | ———————— | |
| ByBlock | ———————— | |
| CENTER2 | —— · —— · —— · | Center (.5x) __ _ __ |
| Continuous | ———————— | Continuous |
| HIDDEN2 | -------------------- | Hidden (.5x) _ _ _ _ _ . |
| PHANTOM2 | —— · · —— · · —— · | Phantom (.5x) __ _ _ |
| PROPERTY-LINE | ----------------- | property-line |

The linetype you created is listed.

Highlight the PROPERTY-LINE linetype and select CURRENT.

9. Draw some lines to see if they look OK. Make sure you make them long enough to see the dashes.

10.  CU963612.dwg          AutoCAD Drawing
     custom-arch.lin       AutoCAD Linetype Definition

Locate the custom-arch.lin file you created.

Open it using NotePad.

11. 
```
custom-arch.lin - Notepad
File  Edit  Search  Help
*PROPERTY-LINE,property-line
A,12,-3,6,-3,6,-3,12
```

You see a description of the property-line.

12. Save as *ex2-2.dwg*.

*Exercise 2-3:*
## Creating a Custom Text Style

Drawing Name:     ex2-2.dwg
Estimated Time:     15 minutes

This exercise reinforces the following skills:

- ❑ Text Styles
- ❑ Customization

Most architects use custom text styles. You may find custom text styles on Autodesk's website using the Design Center, www.cadalog.com, or any number of websites on the Internet. However, the ability to create text styles as needed is an excellent skill for an architectural drafter.

1.    Open or continue working in *ex2-2.dwg*.

2.    Select **Format→Text Style**.

      Table Style...
      Text Style...
      Leader Settings...
      Point Style...

      *You can also type TEXTSTYLE on the command line.*

3.    Press the New button.

4.    Type **Architectural** for the new style name.

      New Text Style
      Style Name:  Architectural    OK
      Cancel

5.    Select **Technic** for the font name.
      Technic is a standard font included with Windows.
      Press **Apply**.
      Then **Close**.

      Font
      Font Name:
      Technic

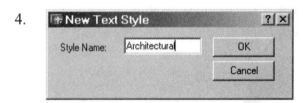

6.  Save the file as 'fonts.dwg' in your custom subdirectory.

File Edit View In
  New...
  Open...
  Close
  Partial Load
  Project Browser...
  Save
  Save As...

Use this drawing to store all your custom text styles. You can then use the Design Center to load any custom fonts from this drawing.

---

**TIP:** MTEXT only uses TrueType fonts.

If you specify an SHX font in MTEXT, it will substitute the TrueType font that Autodesk provides to mimic that SHX font. These mimic fonts are actually very poorly defined. TrueType is intended to always be defined as open outlines, so that the character weight is defined. AutoCAD's SHX-like TrueType fonts (ROMANS.TTF etc) were created by an automatic font generator that faithfully copied the SHX single-stroke form, including the clunky way of using short straight line segments to create curves. This type of definition prevents those TrueType fonts from ever having anything but the minimum stroke-width regardless of character size.

The remedy is: Don't use SHX fonts in MTEXT.

---

*Exercise 2-4:*
## *Creating New Layers*

Drawing Name:      New
Estimated Time:     20 minutes

This exercise reinforces the following skills:

- ❑  Use of toolbars
- ❑  Layer Manager
- ❑  Creating New Layers
- ❑  Loading Linetypes

1.  Start a new drawing using QNEW.

2.  First, we need to load the property-line linetype we defined in Exercise 2-3.

    Launch the Design Center.

3. 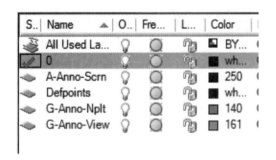 Select the **Folders** tab.

Browse to the folder where you saved the *Ex2-2.dwg* file.

Open the Linetypes folder.

Scroll to the **Property-line** linetype definition.

4. Highlight the PROPERTY-LINE linetype.

Drag and drop into your active window.

5. Close the Design Center.

6. Activate the **Layer Manager**.

Note that several layers have already been created. The template automatically sets your Layer Standards to AIA.

7. Select the **New Layer from Standard** tool.

*If you select the New Layer tool, you won't be able to assign a linetype to the new layer.*

8. 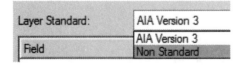 Under Layer Standard, select **Non Standard**.

9.

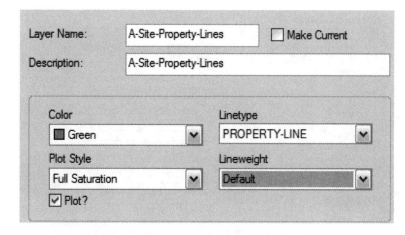

Name the layer **A-Site-Property-Lines**.

Set the Color to **Green**.

Select the **Property-Line** linetype.

Set the Lineweight to **Default**.

Enable **Plot**.

10. Press **Apply**.

11.

Name the layer **A-Contour-Line**.

Set the color to **42**.

12. Select the linetype pane for the new linetype.
Press **Other**.

13. Enable **Show Linetypes in File**.

Highlight **DASHEDX2** and press **OK** to assign it to the selected layer name.

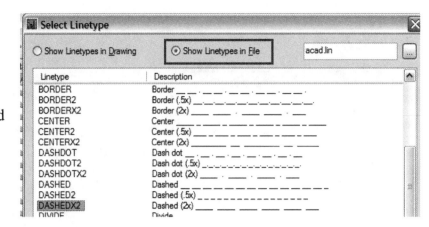

14.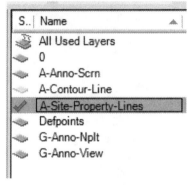

Note that the linetype was assigned properly.

Press **OK**.

15. Current layer: A-Site-Property-Lines : A-Site-Property-Lines

Set the A-Site-Property-Lines layer current.

16. Highlight the layer name then select the green check mark to set current.

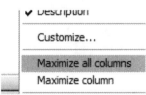

17. Right click on the header bar and select **Maximize all columns** to see all the properties for each layer.

18. Press **Apply** and **OK** to close the Layer Manager.

19. Save as *Ex2-4.dwg*.

*Exercise 2-5:*

## *Transferring a Toolbar*

Drawing Name:     Ex2-4.dwg
Estimated Time:   10 minutes

This exercise reinforces the following skills:

❏  Use of toolbars

1.  Open or continue working in *ex2-4.dwg*.

2.  Type **cui** at the command line.

3.  **Customize User Interface**

    Customize | Transfer

    Select the **Transfer** tab.

4.  Customize | Transfer

    **Customizations in Main CUI**

    Main CUI File (ADT.cui)

    ⚙ Workspaces
    ⊟ Toolbars
       ⊞ Standard
       ⊞ Navigation
       ⊞ Zoom
       ⊞ Views

    Note that you are working in the *ADT.cui* file.

    Expand the *Toolbars* folder.

    These are the toolbars you currently have available.

5.  **Customizations in acad.cui**

    acad.cui

    Locate and open the *acad.cui* file.

6.  ⊟ Toolbars
       ⊞ Dimension
       ⊞ Draw
       ⊞ Draw Order
       ⊞ Inquiry
       ⊞ Insert
       ⊞ Layouts
       ⊞ Modify
       ⊞ Modify II
       ⊞ Properties
       ⊞ Layers
       ⊞ Styles
       ⊞ Object Snap

    Expand the Toolbars folder.

    Note that there are a lot more toolbars available here.

7.		Drag and drop the Styles toolbar from the right-hand list into the left-hand list.

If there are any other toolbars you want to use, drag and drop them over to the ADT.cui side.

8.	Press **Save** to save the changes to the ADT.cui file.
Press **Apply** and **OK** to close.

The Styles toolbar will launch automatically.

*Exercise 2-6:*

## *Creating a Site Plan*

Drawing Name:	Ex2-4.dwg
Estimated Time:	30 minutes

This exercise reinforces the following skills:

- Use of toolbars
- Documentation Tools
- Elevation Marks
- Surveyors' Angles

1.		Open or continue working in *ex2-4.dwg*.

2.	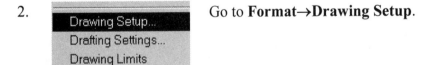	Go to **Format→Drawing Setup**.

3.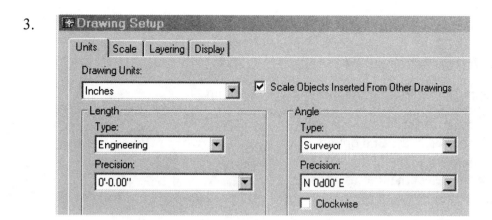

Select the **Units** tab.
Set up the Length Type to **Engineering**.
Set the Precision to **0'-0.00"**.
Set the Angle Type to **Surveyor**.
Set the Precision to **N 0d00' E**.
Press **OK**.

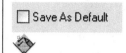

**TIP:** You can set your units as desired and then enable **Save As Default**. Then, all future drawings will use your unit settings.

4.   Draw the property line shown on the **A-Site-Property-Lines** layer.

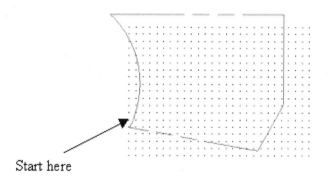

Start here

```
Command: l
LINE Specify first point: 1',50'

Specify next point or [Undo]: @187'<s80de

Specify next point or [Undo]: @75'<n30de

Specify next point or [Close/Undo]: @126'<n

Specify next point or [Close/Undo]: @250'<180
```

This command sequence uses Surveyor's Units.

***Turn ORTHO off before creating the arc.***

Draw an arc using Start, End, Radius to close the figure.

Select the bottom point as the Start point.
Right click and select the End option.
Select the top point at the End point.
Right click and select the Radius option.
The radius is 132'.

(Make sure you use the apostrophe to indicate feet, or your measurements will all be in inches.)

5.   Set the **A-Contour-Line layer** current.

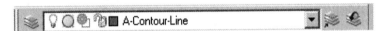

Use the **DIVIDE** command to place points as shown.
The top line is divided into five equal segments.
The bottom-angled line is divided into four equal segments.
The small angled line is divided into two equal segments.

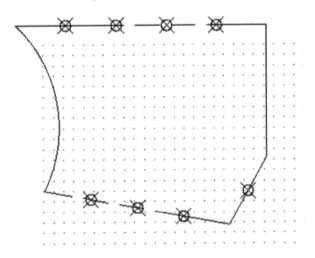

6.

Go to **Format→Point Style** to set the points so they are visible.

Select the Point Style indicated.

Press **OK**.

7. Draw contour lines using **Pline** and **NODE** OSNAPs as shown.

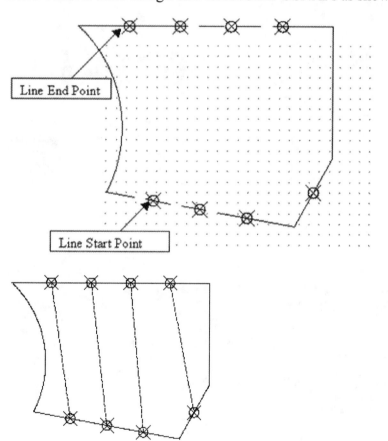

Line End Point

Line Start Point

8. Type **qselect** on the command line.

9.

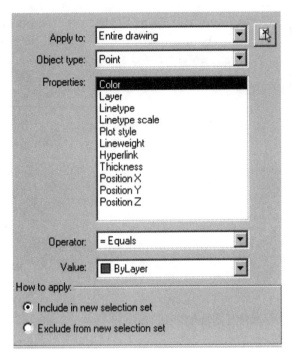

Set the Object Type to **Point**.
Set the Color = Equals **ByLayer**.

Press **OK**.

10. All the points are selected.
Right click and select **Basic Modify Tools→ Delete**.

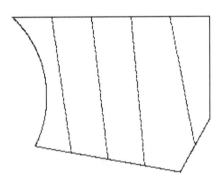

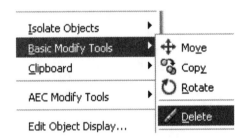

11. Type **Ctl+3** to bring up the Tool Palette.

12. Right click on the Tool Palette bar.

Enable **All Palettes**.

13. Select the **Annotation** Tool Palette.

14. 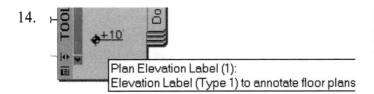 If you scroll down, you'll see an Elevation Label, but it's not the type we need for a site plan.

Instead we'll have to add an elevation label from the Design Center and add it to the Tool Palette.

15. Type **Ctl+2** to launch the Design Center.
Select the AEC Content tab.
Browse to *Imperial/Documentation/Elevation Labels/2D Section.*

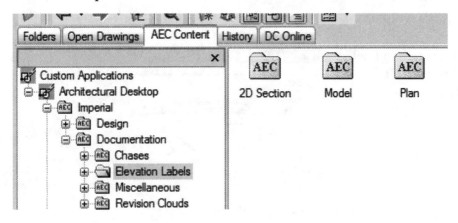

Locate the **Elevation Label (1)** file.

16. 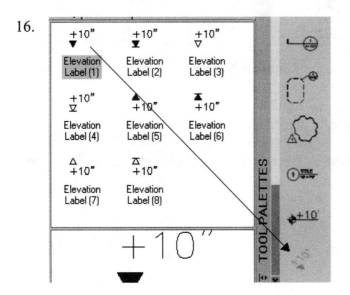 Highlight the elevation label.

Drag and drop onto the Tool Palette.

Close the Design Center.

17.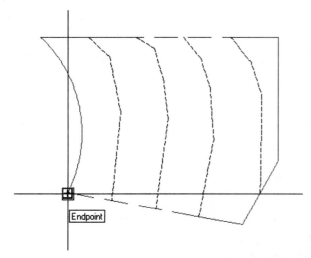

Select the Elevation Label on the Tool Palette.
Select the Endpoint shown.

18. Set the Elevation to **0.00"**.
Set the Prefix to **EL**.
Press **OK**.

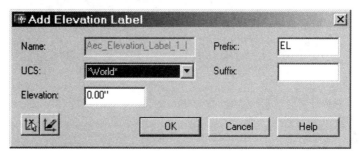

19.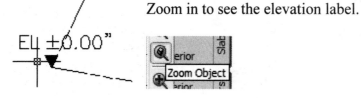

Zoom in to see the elevation label.

You can use the **Zoom Object** tool to zoom in quickly.

A-Anno-Dims     ♀     ✿     🔓   ■ 221

The Elevation Label is automatically placed on the A-Anno-Dims layer.

20. EL ±0.00"

Locate an elevation label on the upper left vertex as shown.

21.

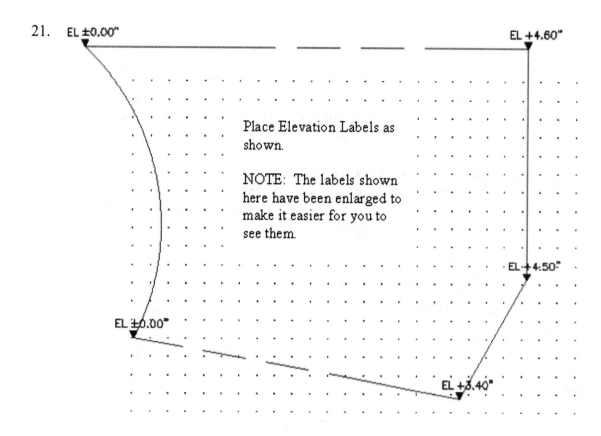

EL ±0.00"  EL +4.60"

Place Elevation Labels as shown.

NOTE: The labels shown here have been enlarged to make it easier for you to see them.

EL +4.50"

EL ±0.00"

EL +3.40"

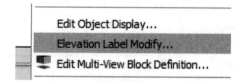

Edit Object Display...

Elevation Label Modify...

Edit Multi-View Block Definition...

To modify the value of the elevation label, select the label.

Right click and select **Elevation Label Modify**.

22. Type **Ctl+2** to launch the Design Center.

Select the Folders tab.
Browse to the *fonts.dwg*. This is the file you created in a previous exercise.

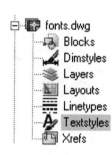

fonts.dwg
Blocks
Dimstyles
Layers
Layouts
Linetypes
Textstyles
Xrefs

23.  Drag and drop the **Architectural** text style into the drawing.

Architectural  Close the Design Center.

24. Set the A-Anno-Dims Layer current.

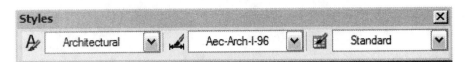

The **Styles** toolbar is located in the *acad.cui* file. If you do not have the toolbar available on the right click menu, you will have to transfer it using the CUI interface. Refer to the previous exercise on how to do this.

Alternatively, you can go to **Format->Textstyle** or type **textstyle** on the command line to set the Architectural font as the current text style.

25. Set **Architectural** as the current text style.

26. Use the **TEXT** command to create the text.
Set the text to 5′ high so you can see it.
Set the rotation angle to −10 degrees
Use %%d to create the degree symbol.

27. EL 1′−10.50″ To create the S60... note, use the **TEXT** command.

Height is 5′, rotation angle is 60 degrees.

*When you are creating the text, it will preview horizontally. However, once you left click or hit ESCAPE to place it, it will automatically rotate to the correct position.*

S 60° W 75.0

EL 1′−5.00″

28. 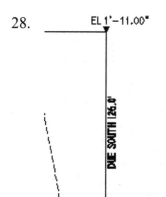 Create the **Due South 126.0′** note using height of 5′, rotation angle of 90 degrees.

29. Add the text shown.

30. 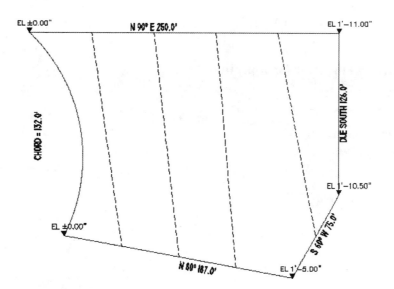 Add the Chord note shown.
Rotation angle is 90 degrees.

31. Save the file as *ex2-6.dwg*.

*Exercise 2-7:*
## Creating a Layer User Group

Drawing Name:      Ex 2-6.dwg
Estimated Time:     15 minutes

This exercise reinforces the following skills:

- ❑ Use of toolbars
- ❑ Layer Manager
- ❑ Layer User Group

A Layer User Group allows you to group your layers, so you can quickly freeze/thaw them, turn them ON/OFF, etc.

---

**TIP:** The difference between FREEZING a Layer and turning it OFF is that entities on FROZEN Layers are not included in REGENS. Speed up your processing time by FREEZING layers.

---

We can create a group of layers that are just used for the site plan and then freeze them when we don't need to see them.

1.      Open *ex2-6.dwg.*

2.      Select the **Layer Manager** tool.

3.      Select the **New Group Filter** tool.

4.      ⊟ All
            All Used Layers
            Site Plan        Name the group **Site Plan**.

5.

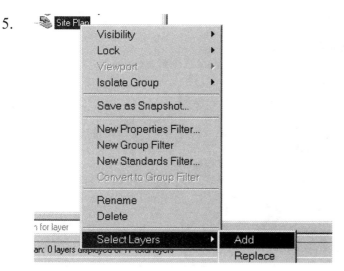

Highlight the Site Plan group.
Right click and select **Select
Layers→Add**.

6. Type **ALL** on the command line.
This selects all the items in the drawing.
The layers are now listed in the Layer Manager under the Site Plan group.

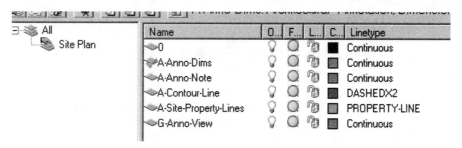

Press **Apply**.

Close the Layer Manager.

7. We can use this group to quickly freeze, turn off, etc. the layers in the Site Plan group.

Save the drawing as *ex2-7.dwg* and close.

**NOTES:**

# QUIZ 1

## *True or False*

1. Doors, windows, and walls are inserted into the drawing as objects.
2. The Architectural Toolbars are loaded from the ADT Menu Group.
3. To set the template used by the QNEW tool, use Options.

4. If you start a New Drawing using 'QNew' tool shown above, the Start-Up dialog will appear unless you assign a template.
5. Mass elements are used to create Mass Models.
6. The Layer Manager is used to organize, sort, and group layers.
7. Layer Standards are set using the Layer Manager.
8. You must load a custom linetype before you can assign it to a layer.

## *Multiple Choice*
### *Select the best answer.*

9. If you start a drawing using one of the standard templates, AutoCAD Architecture will automatically create _____ layouts.

   A. A work layout plus Model Space
   B. Four layouts, plus Model Space
   C. Ten layouts, plus Model Space
   D. Eleven layouts, plus Model Space

10. Options are set through:

   A. Options
   B. Desktop
   C. User Settings
   D. Template

11. The Display Manager controls:

   A. How AEC objects are displayed in the graphics window
   B. The number of viewports
   C. The number of layout tabs
   D. Layers

12. Mass Elements are created using the _____ Tool Palette.

    A. Massing
    B. Concept
    C. General Drafting
    D. Documentation

13. Wall Styles are created by:

    A. Highlighting a Wall on the Wall tab of the Tool Palette, right click and select Wall Styles
    B. Type **WallStyle** on the command line
    C. Go to Format→Style Manager
    D. All of the Above

14. To create a New Layer, use:

    A. Type **LayerManager** at the command line
    B. Type **Layer** at the command line
    C. Use **Format→Layer Management→Layer Manager**
    D. All of the Above

15. You can change the way AEC objects are displayed by using:

    A. Edit Object Display
    B. Edit Display Properties
    C. Edit Entity Properties
    D. Edit AEC Properties

**ANSWERS:**

1) T; 2) T; 3) T; 4) T; 5) T; 6) T; 7) T; 8) T; 9) A; 10) A; 11) A; 12) A; 13) D; 14) D; 15) A

## Lesson 3
# Floor Plans

The floor plan is central to any architectural drawing. We start by placing the exterior walls, then the interior walls, then doors, and finally windows.

| Tool Palette | Walls |
|---|---|
| Command Line | WallAdd |
| Menu | Design→Walls→Add Wall |

### Exercise 3-1:
## *Creating Exterior Walls*

Drawing Name:     New
Estimated Time:    10 minutes

This exercise reinforces the following skills:

- ❑ Create Walls
- ❑ Project Navigator

1.      Start a new drawing using QNEW.

2.      Launch the Tool Palette.

Select the **Walls** tab.

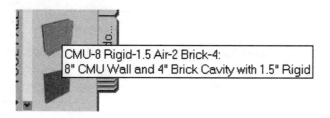

Select the **CMU-8 RIGID-1.5 Air-2 Brick-4:** wall style.

3.        Toggle **ORTHO** ON.

Start the wall at 0,0.
Create a rectangle 60′ tall and 30′ wide.

4.    Select the **Work** tab.

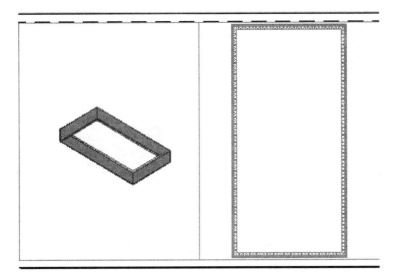

5.    You see that the walls you placed are really 3-dimensional.

6.    Save your drawing as *Ex3-1.dwg.*

---

**TIP:** If you draw a wall and the materials composing the wall are on the wrong side,
you can reverse the direction of the wall. Simply select the wall, right click and select
the Reverse option from the menu.

*Exercise 3-2:*

## Convert to Walls

Drawing Name:     new
Estimated Time:   60 minutes

This exercise reinforces the following skills:

- ❑ Convert to Walls
- ❑ Drawing references (previously known as external references or Xrefs)
- ❑ Creating Interior Walls

1.       Start a new drawing using **QNEW**.

2.     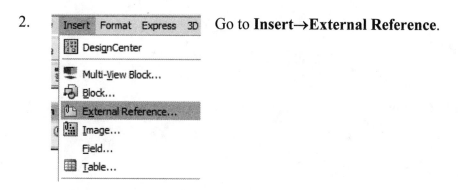   Go to **Insert→External Reference**.

3.     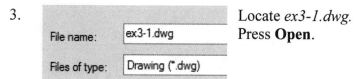   Locate *ex3-1.dwg*.
Press **Open**.

**TIP:** Many architects use external drawing references to organize their projects. That way teams of architects can concentrate just on their portions of a building. External references also use less system resources.

4.

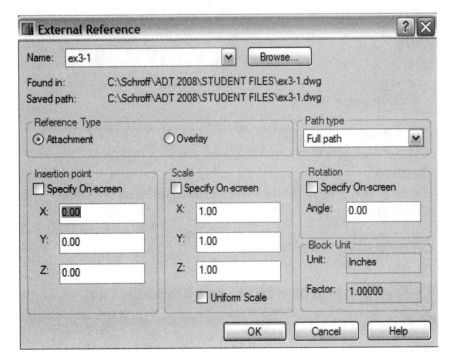

Uncheck **Specify On-Screen** under Insertion point, scale, and rotation.

Press **OK**.
This will insert the file as an external reference at 0,0,0.

---

**TIP:** You can convert lines, arcs, circles, or polylines to walls. If you have created a floor plan in AutoCAD and want to convert it to 3D, open the floor plan drawing inside of AutoCAD Architecture. Use the Convert to Walls tool to transform your floor plan into walls.

5.

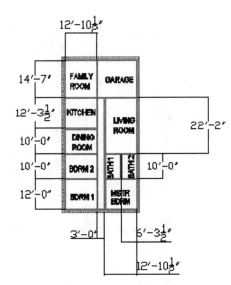

Create the layout shown using lines or polylines.  (It may be helpful to turn off the A-Walls layer while you are working and create your lines on layer 0).

**Do not add the dimensions or the text to your drawing.**  They are there to help you place the lines only.

Don't draw using rectangles if you are going to use the CONVERT method or you will get duplication of lines over lines, which will affect the wall creation.

If you do not want to spend time creating the floor plan, you can download the drawing 'floor plan.dwg' from www.schroff1.com.

6.

Locate the **Stud-4 GWB-0.625 Each Side:** wall style.

7.     Highlight the Wall tool.
Right click and select **Apply Tool Properties to→Linework**.

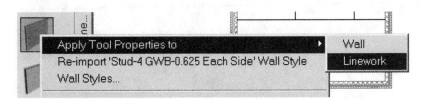

8.     Select all the interior polylines you just created.

```
Erase layout geometry? [Yes/No] <N>: Y

15 new wall(s) created.
Command: Regenerating model.
```

You are prompted if you want to erase the layout geometry.  Type **Y** for Yes.

9.     Switch to the Work tab so you can see how your house looks in 3D.

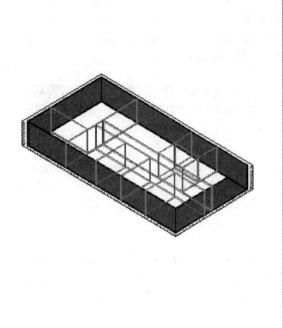 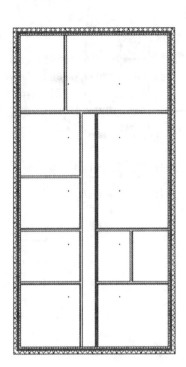

10.  Save the file as *ex3-2.dwg*.

*Exercise 3-3:*
# Wall Cleanup

Drawing Name:     ex3-2.dwg
Estimated Time:    30 minutes

This exercise reinforces the following skills:

- ❏ Modifying Walls
- ❏ Edit Justification
- ❏ Wall Tools
- ❏ Xref Manager
- ❏ Edit External References In-Place
- ❏ Unreconciled Layers

1. 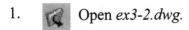 Open *ex3-2.dwg*.

2. 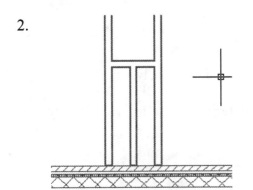      Add a closet area between the master bedroom and Bedroom #1.

    To do this, draw a wall from the mid-point of the wall in the horizontal direction and then draw a vertical wall from the mid-point of the new horizontal wall.

3. 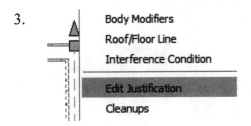      To center the vertical wall, select it.
    Right click and select **Edit Justification**.

    Body Modifiers
    Roof/Floor Line
    Interference Condition
    Edit Justification
    Cleanups

4. 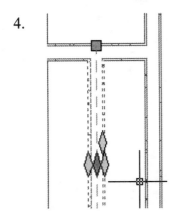      Diamond grips will appear to indicate different wall justification methods (Left/Right/Center).

    Select the Center Diamond.

5.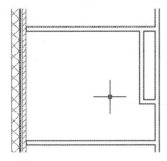

Draw a closet in Bedroom #2.
Use the same interior wall style.
Set the wall 1′ from the hallway wall and 6′ in length.

Draw a vertical line 2′ inside the living room area.

CMU-8 Rigid
-1.5 Air-2 B…

Locate the exterior wall style we used previously.

Convert the vertical line to the exterior wall styles using **Apply Tool Properties to Linework**.

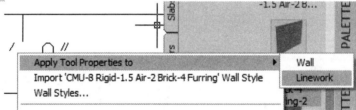

6.

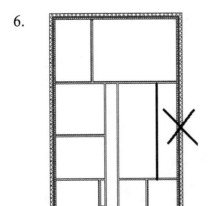

Next, we delete the wall indicated and modify the exterior wall so it creates a porch entry way..

7.

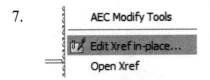

Select the exterior walls.
Right click and select **Edit Xref in-place**.

8.

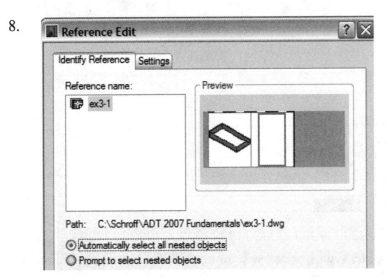

Enable Automatically select all nested objects.

Press **OK**.

By enabling the ability to select nested objects, you would be able to select blocks or other items inserted in the drawing. It is not really applicable here as there are no nested objects…just walls.

You'll notice that the interior walls now appear lighter to allow you to select the referenced file's objects.

9.

Use the Break tool to create the opening for the living room entrance.

10.

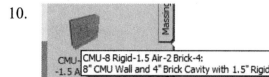

Locate the **CMU-8 Rigid-1.5 Air-2 Brick-4** wall style.

11.

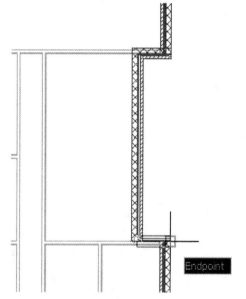

Draw a new wall section indenting 4′ in using the end points of the remaining exterior wall.

12.

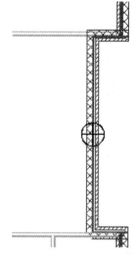

A circle with an 'x' will appear. This indicates a fault error. A fault error occurs when walls over-lap or you have a wall in the wrong direction.

In this case, the wall was drawn in a different direction (note the hatch pattern.) from the other walls.

13. 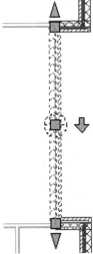 If you select the wall, blue grips appear. The blue arrow indicates the exterior side of the wall.

14. If you select a different wall, you see that the blue arrow is located on the opposite side.

All the walls should have the blue arrow located on the exterior side.

To flip the wall, simply left pick on the blue arrow.

15. The corners may require some clean-up work.

16. 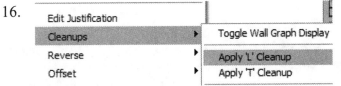 Select a wall.
Right click and select **Apply 'L' Cleanup**.
Then select the adjacent wall.

17. Select the Save and Close Xref tool.

18. 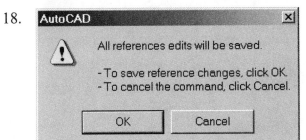 Press **OK**.

You can now edit the interior walls but not the exterior walls.

19. 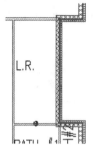 The walls appear cleaner.

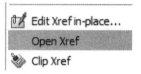

If you have difficulty cleaning up the walls using the 'Edit Xref in-place' option, select the external reference, right click and select 'Open Xref'. This will open up the file you are referencing. Clean up the walls as needed, then save. The drawing hosting the external reference will update.

 You may see a notification that you have unreconciled layers. Unreconciled layers are new layers that have been added to a drawing without user acknowledgement. When you inserted the external reference file, new layers were added to the drawing.

20. Select the layer alert icon in the task tray.

21. 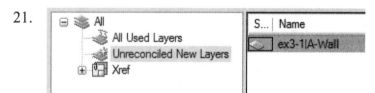 You will see a category for Unreconciled New Layers and the right pane will display a list of the new layers.

22. 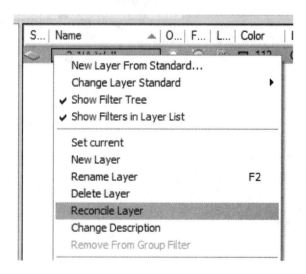 Highlight the layer in the right pane.

Right click and select 'Reconcile Layer'.

23.

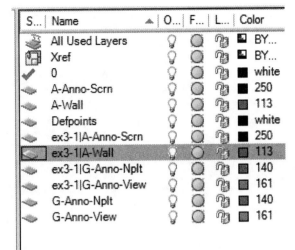

The layer will be added to the Used Layer list.

Press **Apply** and **OK** to exit the Layer Manager dialog.

24.

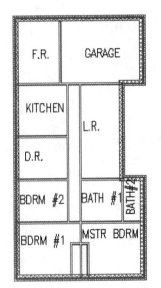

The drawing is now updated.

Save as *ex3-3.dwg*.

*Exercise 3-4:*
## Adding Closet Doors

Drawing Name:      Ex3-3.dwg
Estimated Time:     10 minutes

This exercise reinforces the following skills:

    ❑  Adding Doors
    ❑  Door Properties

1.    Open *ex3-3.dwg.*

2.    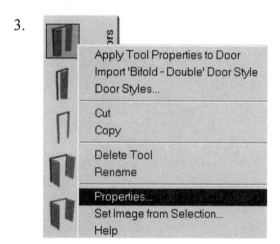    Locate the **Bifold-Double** door on the Doors tab of the Tool Palette.

3.    Highlight the **Bifold-Double** door. Right click and select **Properties**.

---

**TIP:** To create a freestanding door, press the ENTER key when prompted to pick a wall. You can then use the grips on the door entity to move and place the door wherever you like.

To move a door along a wall, use Door→Reposition→Along Wall. Use the OSNAP From option to locate a door a specific distance from an adjoining wall.

---

4.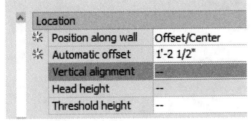

Expand the **Dimensions** section.
Set the Standard sizes to
**5'-0" x 6'-8"**.

---

**TIP:** If you left click in the field, a down arrow will appear...select the down arrow and you will get a list of standard sizes. Then, select the size you want.

---

Set the Opening percentage to **50**.

A 25% opening will show a door swing at a 45-degree angle.
The value of the Opening percentage determines the angle of the arc swing.
A 50% value indicates the door will appear half-open at a 90-degree angle.

5.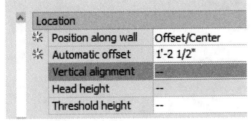

Expand the **Location** section.

Set Position along wall to **Offset/Center**.

Set the Automatic offset to **1'-2 1/2"**.

(This will center the closet doors along the wall.)

Press **OK** to close the Properties dialog.

---

**TIP:** Note the vertical alignment field. It defaults to a threshold height of 0" for doors and a head height of 6'8" for windows. You will need to adjust these defaults in multi-story buildings.

---

6.    Place the Bifold Double doors at the two closets.

The orientation of the door swing is determined by the wall side selected. In both cases, you want to select the outside face of the wall.

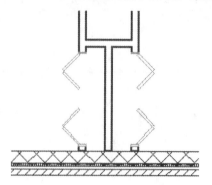

7.    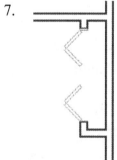    Place a Bi-fold Double door in the wall shown.

8.    Save as *ex3-4.dwg*.

*Exercise 3-5:*
## Adding Interior Doors

Drawing Name:  ex3-4.dwg
Estimated Time:  10 minutes

This exercise reinforces the following skills:

- ❑ Adding Doors
- ❑ Door Properties

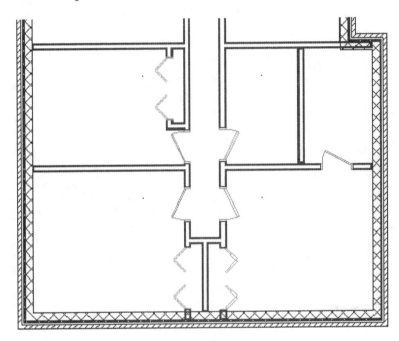

We will add single hinge doors in the areas shown.

You may need to do some wall cleanup to get the rooms to look proper.

Use AddWall, Extend, and Trim as needed.

Try to keep the walls so they line up to keep the floor plan looking clean.

1.  Open *ex3-4.dwg*.

2.  Locate the **Single Hinged** door on the Doors tab of the Tool Palette. Right click and select **Properties**.

3.

| Bound spaces | By style |
|---|---|
| **Dimensions** | |
| Standard sizes | 2'-6" X 8'-0" |
| A Width | 2'-6" |
| B Height | 8'-0" |
| Measure to | Inside of frame |
| Swing angle | 25 |

Expand the Dimensions section.
Set the Standard sizes to
**2'-6" x 8'-0"**.
Set the Swing angle to **25**.

4.

| **Location** | |
|---|---|
| Position along wall | Offset/Center |
| Automatic offset | 6" |
| Vertical alignment | Threshold |
| Head height | 7'-0" |
| Threshold height | 0" |
| Rotation | 0.00 |

Set the Position along wall to **Offset/ Center**.
Set the Automatic offset to **6"**.

Press **OK**.

5. Place the doors as indicated on the previous page.

6. Save the file *ex3-5.dwg*.

*Exercise 3-6:*

# Add Opening

Drawing Name:      ex3-5.dwg
Estimated Time:     15 minutes

This exercise reinforces the following skills:

- ❑ Adding Openings
- ❑ Opening Properties
- ❑ Copying Tools
- ❑ Set Image from Selection

Openings can be any size and elevation. They can be applied to a wall or be freestanding. Openings are placed on Layer A-Wall-Open. The Add Opening Properties allow the user to either select a Pre-defined shape for the opening or use a custom shape.

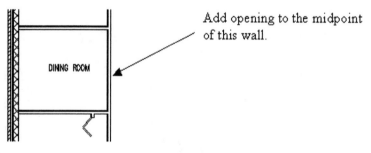

Add opening to the midpoint of this wall.

DINING ROOM

1. 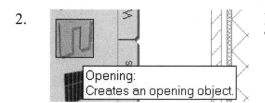 Open *ex3-5.dwg.*

2.  Locate the **Opening** on the Design tab of the Tool Palette.

## Copy a Tool

3. 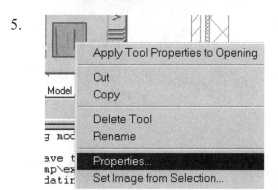 Right click and select **Copy**.

4. 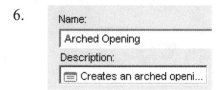 Select the **Doors** tab.
Right click and select **Paste**.

5.  Highlight the copied tool.
Right click and select **Properties**.

6. Change the Name to **Arched Opening**.
Change the Description to **Creates an arched opening object**.

Expand the General section.
Set the Description to **Creates an Arched Opening**.
Set the Layer key to **OPENING**.
Set the Shape to **Arch**.

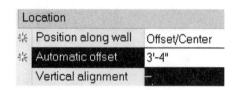

Expand the Dimensions section.
Set the Width to **3'-0"**.
Set the Height to **6'-8"**.
Set the Rise to **1'-0"**.

Expand the Location section.
Set the Position along wall to **Offset/Center**.
Set the Automatic offset to **3'-4"**.

Press **OK**.

7.   Place the arched opening in the dining room wall.

8.   Use **View→3D orbit** to view the arched opening.

## Create an Image for a Tool

9.   Select the Arched Opening icon.
Right click and select **Set Image from Selection…**
Pick the arched opening you created.

The icon updates to show an arched opening.

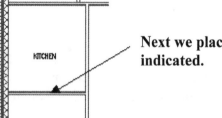

**Next we place a rectangular opening in the location indicated.**

10.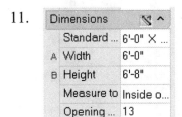

Select the **Cased Opening** tool from the Doors Tool Palette.

11.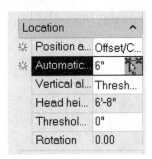

Expand the Dimensions section.
Set the Width to **6'-0"**.
Set the Height to **6'-8"**.

Expand the Location section.
Set the Position along wall to **Offset/Center**.
Set the Automatic offset to **6"**.

12.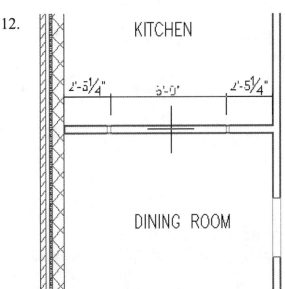

Place the opening in the wall between the kitchen and the dining room.

13.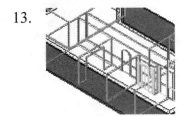

Select the **Work** tab to view the openings.

Select the **Model** tab.

14.

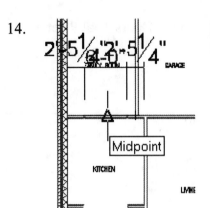

Place a rectangular opening between the kitchen and the family room.

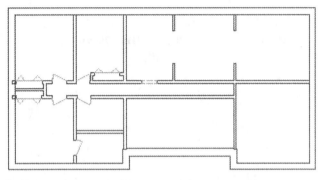

This is our floor plan so far.

The view is set to Low Detail and rotated 90 degrees.

15. Save the file as *ex3-6.dwg*.

*Exercise 3-7:*
## Adding Doors

Drawing Name:     ex3-6.dwg
Estimated Time:   20 minutes

This exercise reinforces the following skills:

❑   Adding Doors

1.   Open *ex3-6.dwg*.

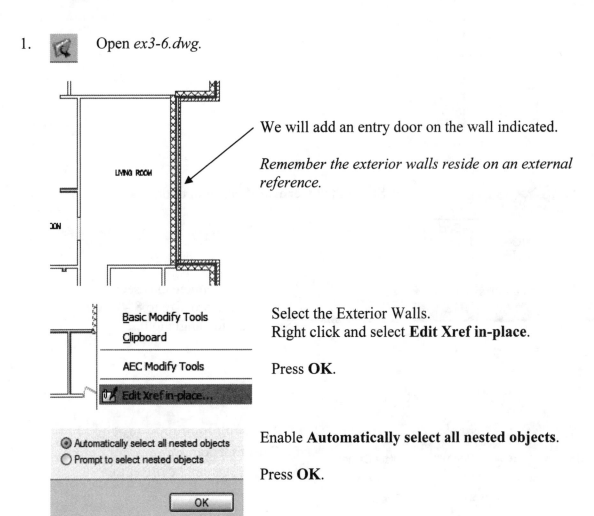

We will add an entry door on the wall indicated.

*Remember the exterior walls reside on an external reference.*

Select the Exterior Walls.
Right click and select **Edit Xref in-place**.

Press **OK**.

Enable **Automatically select all nested objects**.

Press **OK**.

2.   Select the **Hinged-Double-Exterior** door.

3. 

| Dimensions | | |
|---|---|---|
| Standard ... | 4'-0" X ... | |
| A | Width | 4'-0" |
| B | Height | 6'-8" |
| Measure to | Inside o... | |
| Swing an... | 0 | |

Expand the Dimensions section.
Set the Standard size to **4'-0" x 6'-8"**.
Set the Swing angle to **0**.

Expand the Location section.
Set the Position along wall to **Offset/Center**.
Set the Automatic offset to **6"**.

4.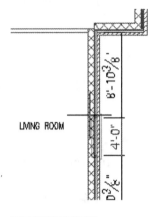

Place the door so it is centered in the wall.

5.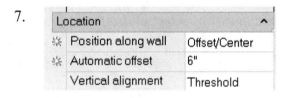

Select the **Overhead-Sectional** door.

6. 

| Dimensions | | |
|---|---|---|
| Standard sizes | 8'-0" X 7'-0" | ▼ |
| A | Width | 8'-0" |
| B | Height | 7'-0" |
| Measure to | Inside of frame | |
| Opening percent | 0 | |

Expand the Dimensions section.
Set the Standard size to **8'-0" x 7'-0"**.
Set the Swing angle to **0**.

7. 

| Location | | |
|---|---|---|
| Position along wall | Offset/Center | |
| Automatic offset | 6" | |
| Vertical alignment | Threshold | |

Set the Position along wall to
**Offset/Center**.
Set the Automatic offset to **6"**.

8.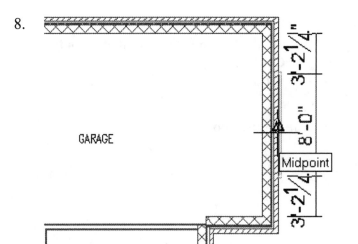

Place the door in the garage wall.

9.

Switch to the Work tab to view the garage door and front entry door.

Switch back to the Model tab.

10. Next we add a sliding door to the family room wall indicated.

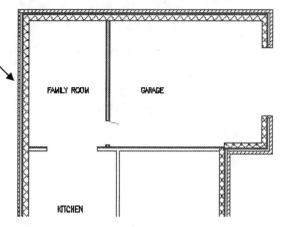

11. Select a **Sliding Door –Double Full Lite** to add to the family room.

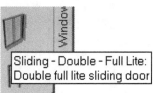

12.

| Dimensions | |
|---|---|
| Standard sizes | 8'-0" × 7'-0" |
| A Width | 8'-0" |
| B Height | 7'-0" |
| Measure to | Inside of frame |
| Opening percent | 0 |

Set the Standard Size to **8'-0" x 7'-0"**.
Set the Opening percent to **0**.

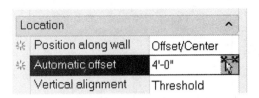

Expand the Location section.
Set the Position along wall to **Offset/Center**.
Set the Automatic offset to **4'-0"**.

13.

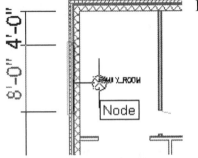

Place the sliding door.

14.

Save the changes back to the external reference.

15.

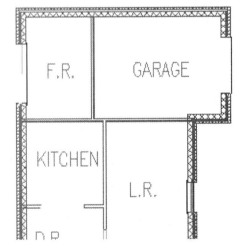

Press **OK**.

16.

If your doors don't look proper, use the Display Manager to modify the appearance.

17.

Go to **Format→Display Manager**.

18. 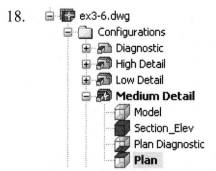 Expand the Configurations folder.

Locate the Plan configuration under Medium Detail.

Note that this configuration is in bold because it is the current active configuration.

19. 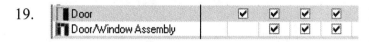 Place a check mark for Doors and Door/Window Assembly to set them visible in all views.

Press **Apply** and **OK**.

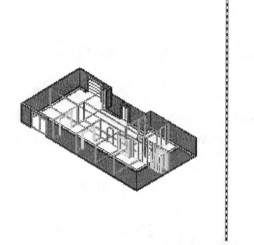 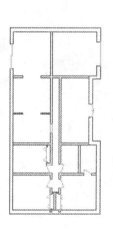

20. Select the Work tab to view your model.

21. Save the file as *ex3-7.dwg*.

## Exercise 3-8:
# Add Window Assemblies

Drawing Name:      Lesson 3-7.dwg
Estimated Time:     30 minutes

This exercise reinforces the following skills:

❑   Add Windows

1.      Open *ex3-7.dwg*.

Select the Model tab.

2.      Select an exterior wall.
Right click and select **Edit Xref In-place**.

Press **OK**.

3.      Select the Windows tab of the Tool Palette.
Select the **Casement-Double** window.

4.      Expand the Dimensions section.
Set the size to **2'-10" x 3'-0"**.

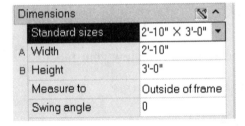

5.      Expand the Location section.
Set the Position along wall to **Offset/Center**.
Set the Offset to **4'-0"**.
Set the Head height to **4'-8"**.

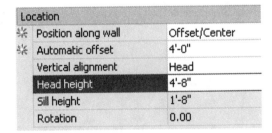

6.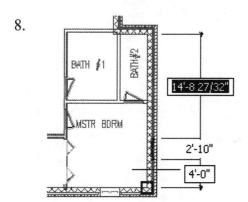

Select the wall shown and the endpoint indicated.

The endpoint is where the offset is calculated from.

7. Select the **Casement-Double** window again.

8.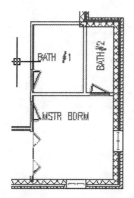

Place the window on the vertical master bedroom wall.

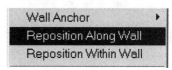

Remember – if you don't like the position of any of the Windows, you can reposition them. Just select the window, right click, and select 'Reposition Along Wall.'

9.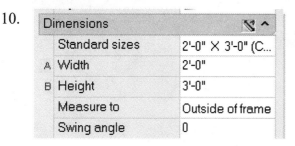

Select the **Casement: Single Casement** window.

10.

| Dimensions | |
| --- | --- |
| Standard sizes | 2'-0" ✕ 3'-0" (C... |
| A Width | 2'-0" |
| B Height | 3'-0" |
| Measure to | Outside of frame |
| Swing angle | 0 |

Expand the Dimensions section.
Set the size to **2'-0" x 3'-0"**.

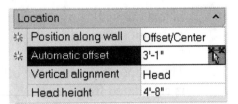

Expand the Location section.
Set the Position along wall to **Offset/ Center**.
Set the Offset to **3'-1"**.

11.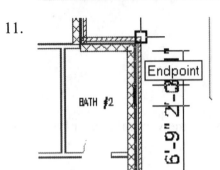

Place the window in the master bath wall.

12. Place a 2'-10" x 3'-0" Double Casement window in Bedroom #1 using a 4'-8" offset.

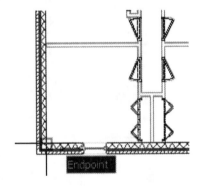

13.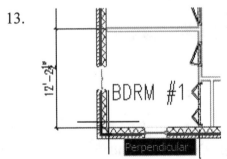

Place a 2'-10" x 3'-0" Double Casement window in Bedroom #1 using a 4'-8" offset on the left vertical wall.

14.

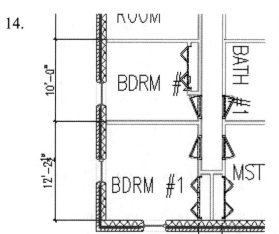

Place a 2'-10" x 3'-0" Double Casement window in Bedroom #2 using a 6'-8" offset on the left vertical wall.

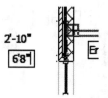

A small edit field will appear when you select the wall to place a window that allows you to change the size of offset on the fly.

15.

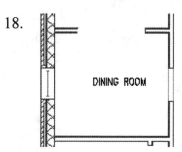

Locate the **Picture- Arched** to place in the left dining room wall.

16.

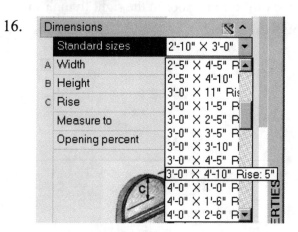

Expand the Dimensions section.
Set the size to **2'-10" x 4'-10" Rise 5"**.

17.

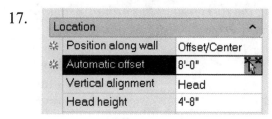

Expand the Location section.
Set the Position along wall to **Offset/Center**.
Set the Offset to **8'-0"**.

18.

Place the window.

19.

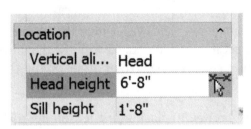

Add a 2'-0" x 3'-0" **Casement: Single** window using a **9'-2"** offset to the kitchen.

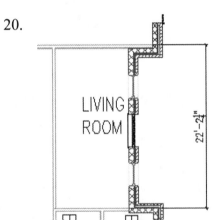

Set the Head height to **6'8"**.

This will ensure that any cabinetry in the kitchen does not interfere with the window.

20.

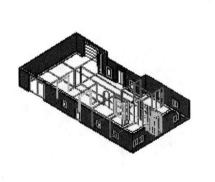

Place an **3'-0" x 4' 6" Rise 5" Arched Picture** window with an offset of 0" on each side of the entry door in the right living room wall.

21.  Select the Save Edits tool.
Press OK to save the modifications to your drawing.

*If Wall Defect symbols appear, try reversing the direction of the wall or using the Wall Cleanup tools. That should eliminate any errors.*

22.

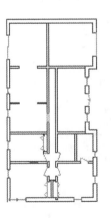

Your floor plan should look similar to the one shown here.

Save as *ex3-8.dwg*.

*Exercise 3-9:*
## Adding a Fireplace

Drawing Name:     ex3-8.dwg
Estimated Time:   30 minutes

This exercise reinforces the following skills:

- ❑  Using the Design Center
- ❑  Adding Openings

In this exercise, we add a fireplace to the family room. You can download the fireplace from the publisher's website or use the fireplace available from the Design Center.

1.  Open *ex3-8.dwg.*

    Select the Model tab.

2.  Select the **Design Center** tool or type **ADC** on the command line.

3.  Select the **DC Online** tab.

    *Note: In order to access DC Online, you must have an active internet connection. If you do not have an active connection, you can download the file from the publisher's website and come back to this exercise.*

4.  In the *Standard Parts* section, browse to **Fireplaces** under *3D Architectural/House Design*.

5.  There is a 3D model with a Hearth.

6.  Hover the mouse over the file icon. An eyedropper will appear. This means the content is idrop-enabled. Simply hold down your left mouse button to fill the eyedropper, then keep the left mouse button down, move the mouse into the graphics window and release the left mouse button to drag and drop the symbol into the drawing file.

7. 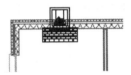 Place the fireplace into the family room wall.

8. 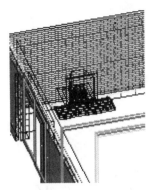 Use the 3D Orbit tool to inspect how the fireplace appears.

Go back to a plan view.

9. 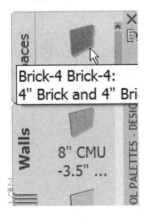 Go to the Walls Tool Palette.

Select the Brick-4 Brick-4 wall style.

10. 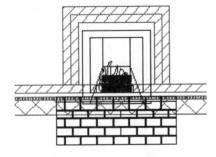 Draw a wall 3′ 4″ in the vertical direction and 4′ 8″ in the horizontal direction to enclose the hearth.

11. 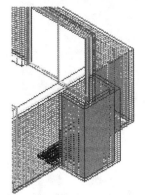 Switch to a NE Isometric view to inspect the chimney.

12. 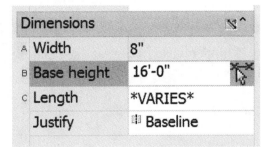 We need to make the chimney taller.

Select the walls for the chimney that were just placed.

Right click and select **Properties**.

13.

| Dimensions | | |
|---|---|---|
| A Width | 8" | |
| B Base height | 16'-0" | |
| C Length | *VARIES* | |
| Justify | Baseline | |

Under Dimensions:

Set the Base Height to **16′**.

14. 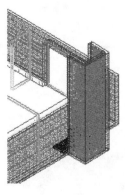 The chimney now looks better.

Switch back to a plan view.

15. 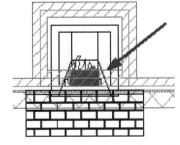 Place a small section of wall to enclose the chimney.

16. Select the wall for the chimney that was just placed.

Right click and select **Properties**.

17.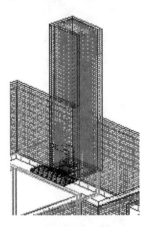

Under Location:

Set the Elevation to **8′**.

18.

Use 3D Orbit to inspect your work so far.

19.

If you switch to a 3D hidden visual style, you see that we need an opening in our fireplace.

Switch back to a plan view.

20.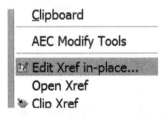

Select the wall where the fireplace is placed.

Right click and select **Edit Xref in-place**.

21.

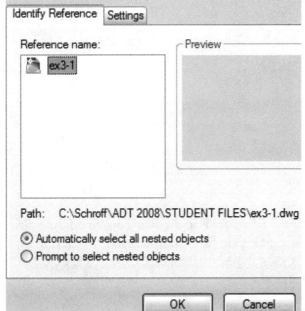

Press **OK**.

22. 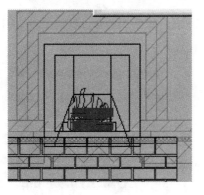  Select the **Opening** tool from the Design Palette.

23.

| Dimensions | |
|---|---|
| A Width | 3'-0" |
| B Height | 2'10" |

Change the Height to **2′ 10″**.

24.

Place the opening in the wall.

25.

Use 3D Orbit and Zoom to inspect the opening in the fireplace.

26.

Use the Add tool to add the chimney and fireplace to the external reference.

27.

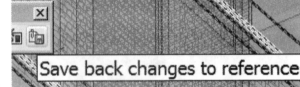

Select the Save icon to save the change to the external reference.

28.

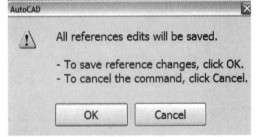

Press **OK**.

29.

Your finished fireplace and chimney should look similar to this.

Save the file as *ex3-9.dwg*.

Close all open drawings.
You can do this by typing **CLOSEALL** on the command line.

# QUIZ 2

## *True or False*

1. The two types of Layer Filter Groups are Dynamic and Stationary.

2. You can create Layer Filter Groups using the Layer Style Manager Dialog.

3. A Snapshot saves the layer settings.

4. Once a door or window is placed, it can not be moved or modified.

5. Openings can be any size and any elevation.

6. The Offset value when placing a door/window/opening determines how far the door/window/opening is placed from a selected point.

7. Door, window and opening dimensions can be applied using the Design Center.

## *Multiple Choice*

8. Select the entity type that can NOT be converted to a wall:

    A. Line
    B. Polyline
    C. Circle
    D. Spline

9. Doors are automatically placed on this layer:

    A. A-OPENING
    B. A-DOOR
    C. A-WINDOW
    D. A-WALL-OPENING

10. A HOT grip is indicated by this color:

    A. GREEN
    B. BLUE
    C. RED
    D. YELLOW

11. Openings are placed on this layer:

    A. A-OPENING
    B. A-DOOR
    C. A-WINDOW
    D. A-WALL-OPEN


12. To assign an image to a tool on the tool palette using existing geometry, use

    A. Assign image
    B. Set Image from selection
    C. Insert
    D. Import

**ANSWERS:**

1) F; 2) T 3) T; 4) F; 5) T; 6) T; 7) F; 8) C; 9) B; 10) C; 11) A; 12) B

## Lesson 4
# Space Planning

A residential structure is divided into three basic areas:

- ❑ Bedrooms: Used for Sleeping and Privacy
- ❑ Common Areas: Used for gathering and entertainment, such as family rooms and living rooms, and dining area
- ❑ Service Areas: Used to perform functions, such as the kitchen, laundry room, garage, and storage areas

When drawing your floor plan, you need to verify that enough space is provided to allow placement of items, such as beds, tables, entertainment equipment, cars, stoves, bathtubs, lavatories, etc.

AutoCAD Architecture comes with Design Content to allow designers to place furniture to test their space. Additional architectural content is provided at no charge from the Schroff Development Corporation's website at www.schroff1.com for readers of this textbook.

### *Exercise 4-1:*
## *Creating AEC Content*

Drawing Name:     new
Estimated Time:     20 minutes

This lesson reinforces the following skills:

- ❑ Design Center
- ❑ AEC Content
- ❑ Customization

1.     🗔     Start a new drawing using **QNEW**.

2.     Type **XREF** on the command line.

3. 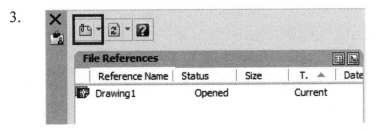     Select **Attach**.

4.

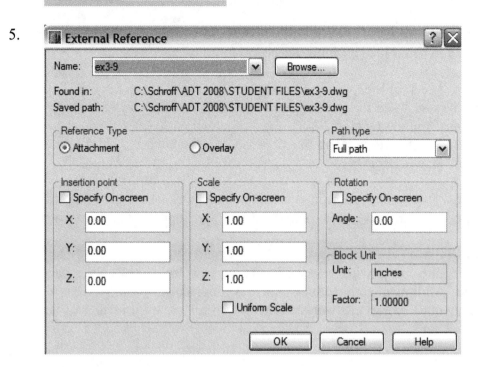

Browse for *ex3-9.dwg* and press Open.

5.

Accept the defaults and press **OK**.

The palette lists the file references now loaded in the drawing.

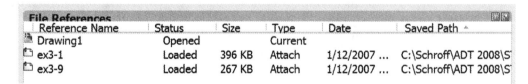

6. Zoom Extents

7. Launch the Design Center.

8.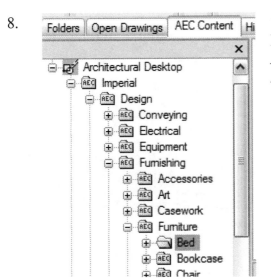

Select the AEC Content tab.
Browse to *AutoCAD Architecture/Imperial/Design/Furnishing/ Furniture/Bed.*

9.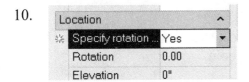

Select the *King.dwg* file.
Right click and select **Insert**.

10.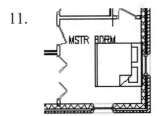

Set Specify rotation to **Yes** in the Properties dialog.

11.

Place the bed in the master bedroom.

12.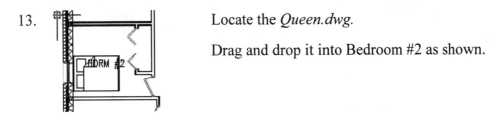

Select the bed.

Note that the bed was automatically placed on the I-Furn layer.

13.

Locate the *Queen.dwg.*

Drag and drop it into Bedroom #2 as shown.

14.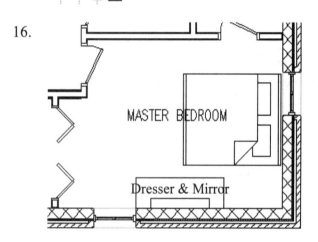

Locate the *Twin.dwg* and place it in Bedroom#1.

15.

Browse to the *Accessories* folder in the Design Center.

16.

Dresser &
Mirror

Place a Dresser & Mirror in the master bedroom.

17.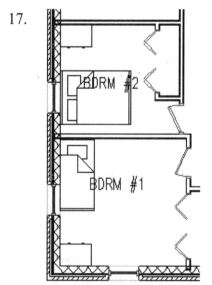

Dresser

Add a dresser to each of the smaller bedrooms.

18.

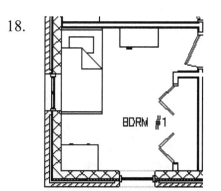

36x18 Left

Locate the *36x18 Left.dwg* file under the *Desk* folder. Place into Bedroom #1.

19.

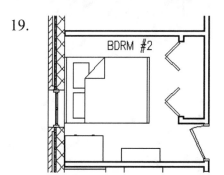

6 Shelves

Locate the *6 Shelves,dwg* bookcase in the *Bookcase* folder.
Place in Bedroom #2.

20.

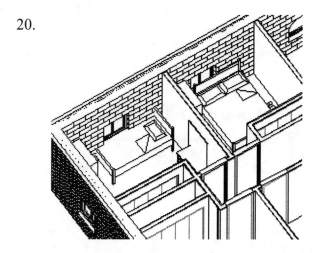

Switch to a 3D view and use 3D Orbit to view the furniture placement.

21.   Save as *ex4-1.dwg*.

*Exercise 4-2:*
## Equipping the Bathrooms

Drawing Name:    Ex4-1.dwg
Estimated Time:   30 minutes

This lesson reinforces the following skills:

- ☐ Design Center
- ☐ Tool Palette
- ☐ Customization

1. Open *ex4-1.dwg*.

   Select the Model tab.
   Switch to a top view.

2. Launch the Design Center.

3. Launch the Tool Palette

## Creating a Tool Palette

4. Select the bottom of the Tool Palette below the expand/contract arrows.
   Right click and select **New Palette**.

5. Pick the New Palette tab.
   Right click and select **Rename Palette**.

6. 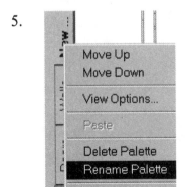 Type **Plumbing**.

7.

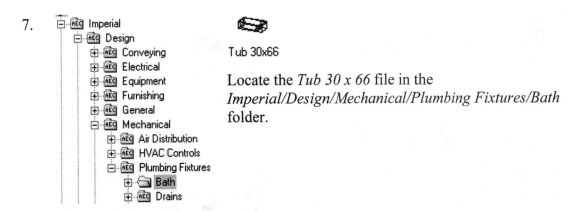

Tub 30x66

Locate the *Tub 30 x 66* file in the *Imperial/Design/Mechanical/Plumbing Fixtures/Bath* folder.

8.

Drag and drop the *Tub 30 x 66* onto the Plumbing Palette. You can release when you see the bar as shown.

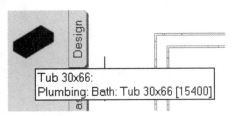

9.

Tank 2

Locate *Tank 2* in the Toilet folder.
Drag and drop onto the Plumbing Palette.

10.

32x34

Locate the *32 x 34* shower in the shower folder.
Drag and drop onto the Plumbing Palette.

*You change how icons appear on the Tool Palette by using the View options.*

11.

Vanity

Locate the *Vanity* in the *Lavatory* folder.
Drag and drop onto the Plumbing Palette.

Close the Design Center.

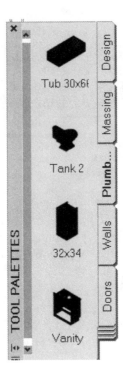

## Adding Fixtures to Bathrooms

12.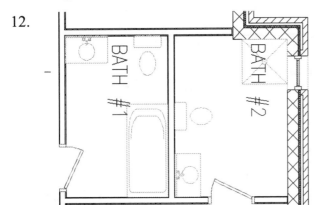

Using the tools on the new
Plumbing Palette, equip the two
bathrooms as shown.

13. Select the tub.

Note that the plumbing fixtures were automatically
placed on the *P-Flor-Fixt* layer.

14. Save as *ex4-2.dwg*.

**TIP:** The Space Planning process is not just to ensure that the rooms can hold the
necessary equipment, but also requires the drafter to think about plumbing, wiring, and
HVAC requirements based on where and how items are placed.

*Exercise 4-3:*
## Changing the Icons on a Tool Palette

Drawing Name:     new
Estimated Time:   5 minutes

This lesson reinforces the following skills:

    □  Tool Palette
    □  Customization

1.      Start a new drawing using **QNEW**.

2.    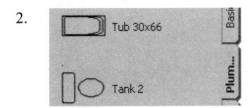    Select the **Plumbing** tab on the Tool Palette.

3.    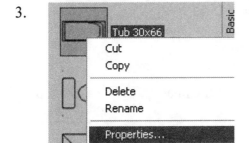    Highlight the Tub tool.

    Right click and select **Properties**.

---

**TIP:** As an additional exercise, place towel bars, soap dishes and other items in the bathrooms.

4.

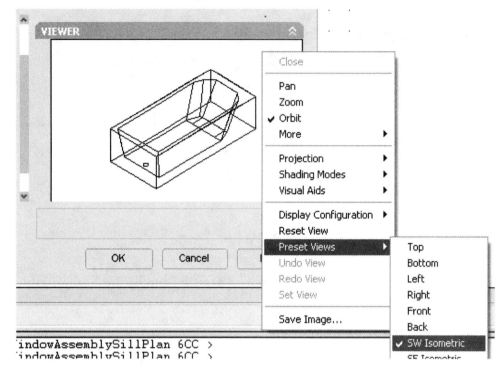

Scroll down to the Viewer section of the dialog.
Right mouse click in the graphics window area.
Select **Preset Views→SW Isometric**.
The display will shift to the selected view.

5.

Place your mouse over the image preview at the top of the dialog.

Right click and select **Refresh Image**.

6.  Close the file without saving. The icons in your tool palette will retain their settings.

**Exercise 4-4:**
## Furnishing the Common Areas

Drawing Name:     Ex4-2.dwg
Estimated Time:   30 minutes

Common areas are the Living Room, Dining Room, and Family Room.

This lesson reinforces the following skills:

    ❑  Design Center
    ❑  Tool Palette
    ❑  Customization

*You will need Internet access in order to complete this exercise.*

1.    Open *ex4-2.dwg*.

   Select the Model tab.
   Switch to a top view.

2.    Launch the Design Center.

3.    Launch the Tool Palette

## Creating a Tool Palette

4.     New Palette

       Rename Palette Set

               Select the bottom of the Tool Palette below the expand/contract arrows.
   Right click and select **New Palette**.

5.     Move Up

       Move Down

       View Options...

       Paste

       Delete Palette

       Rename Palette

               Pick the New Palette tab.
   Right click and select **Rename Palette**.

6. 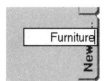 Rename the Tool Palette **Furniture**.

## Adding Tools from Design Center Online

7. 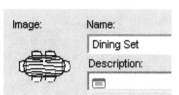 In the Design Center dialog, select the DC Online tab.

Browse to *3D Architecture/Furniture/ Tables*.

8. 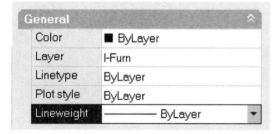 Drag and drop the file called **DINOVL72** onto the new palette. There may be slight pause while the file downloads from Autodesk's sever.

9. Select the DNOVL72 tool.
   Right click and select **Properties**.

Change the name to Dining Set.

Scroll down and expand the General section.
Set Color to **ByLayer**.
Set the Layer to **I-Furn**.
Set Linetype to **ByLayer**.
Set Plot Style to **ByLayer**.
Set Lineweight to **ByLayer**.

10.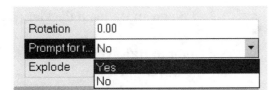

Set the Prompt for rotation to **Yes**.

Press **OK** to close the Properties dialog.

11.

Browse to *3D Architecture/Furniture/Chairs* folder.

Drag and drop the **loungrnd** chair onto the Furniture Palette.

Select the LOUNGRND tool.
Right click and select **Properties**.

Change the name to **Lounge Chair**.

12.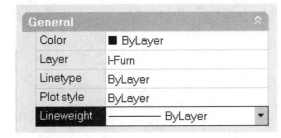

Scroll down and expand the General section.
Set Color to **ByLayer**.
Set the Layer to **I-Furn**.
Set Linetype to **ByLayer**.
Set Plot Style to **ByLayer**.
Set Lineweight to **ByLayer**.

13.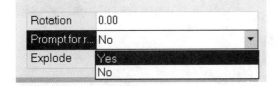

Set the Prompt for rotation to **Yes**.

Press **OK** to close the Properties dialog.

14.

Browse to *3D Architecture/Furnishings/Sofas* folder.

Drag and drop the **loveset6** onto the Furniture Palette.

Select the LOVESET6 tool.
Right click and select **Properties**.

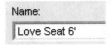

Change the Name to **Love Seat 6′**.

15.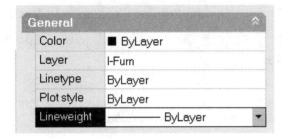

Scroll down and expand the General section.
Set Color to **ByLayer**.
Set the Layer to **I-Furn**.
Set Linetype to **ByLayer**.
Set Plot Style to **ByLayer**.
Set Lineweight to **ByLayer**.

16.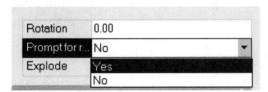

Set the Prompt for rotation to **Yes**.

17.

Browse to *3D Architecture/Furniture/Tables* folder.

Drag and drop the **tblcoffe** onto the Furniture Palette.

Select the TBLCOFFE tool.
Right click and select **Properties**.

18.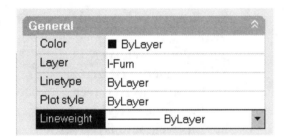

Scroll down and expand the General section.
Set the Layer to **I-Furn**.
Set Color to **ByLayer**.
Set Linetype to **ByLayer**.
Set Plot Style to **ByLayer**.
Set Lineweight to **ByLayer**.

19.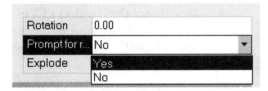

Set the Prompt for rotation to **Yes**.

20.

Browse to *3D Architecture/Furniture/Entertainment Center* folder.

Drag and drop the **entcntr** onto the Furniture Palette.

Select the ENTCNTR tool.
Right click and select **Properties**.

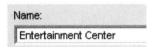

Change the Name to **Entertainment Center**.

21.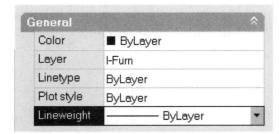

Scroll down and expand the General section.
Set the Layer to **I-Furn**.
Set Color to **ByLayer**.
Set Linetype to **ByLayer**.
Set Plot Style to **ByLayer**.
Set Lineweight to **ByLayer**.

22.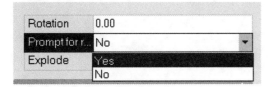

Set the Prompt for rotation to **Yes**.

This is what your Furniture Tool Palette should look like.

*If you have difficulty copying from the Design Center to the Tool Palette, you can download all these files from the publisher's website.*

*Then drag and drop onto the Tool Palette using the Folders tab on the Design Center.*

23. Close the Design Center.

24.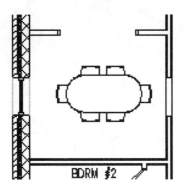

Add the **DINOVL72** to the dining room.

25. 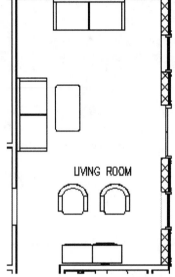 Furnish the living room with the lounge chair, sofa, coffee table, and entertainment center.

26. 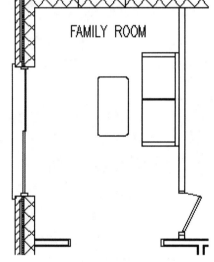 Add a sofa and coffee table to the family room.

27. Save the file as *ex4-4.dwg*.

*Exercise 4-5*
## Adding to the Service Areas

Drawing Name:    Ex4-4.dwg
Estimated Time:    30 minutes

1.    Open *ex4-4.dwg.*

    Select the Model tab.
    Switch to a top view.

2.    Launch the Design Center.

3.            Select the AEC Content tab.
    Browse to the *AutoCAD Architecture/Imperial/ Design/Site/Basic Site/Vehicles* folder.

4.    Drag and drop the *Compact* car into the garage.

5.    If you pick the car, you see that it is placed on the *C-Site-Vhcl* layer automatically.

**TIP:** If the preview shown in the Design Center does not appear as a 3D object, then it is a 2D object. Don't select it for use in your model.

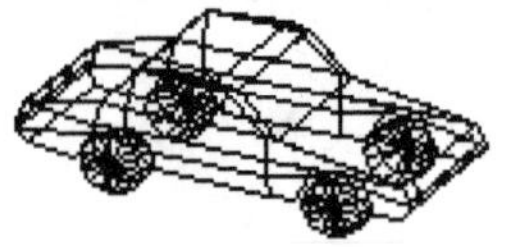

All that remains is the kitchen area.

6. 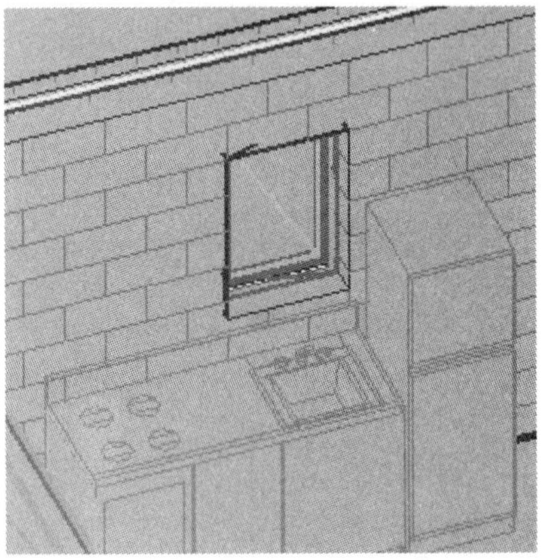

Use the Design Center to add casework, a kitchen sink, and an oven into the kitchen area.

You may need to reposition the window so it is over the sink. To do this, use the **Edit Xref In Place** option.

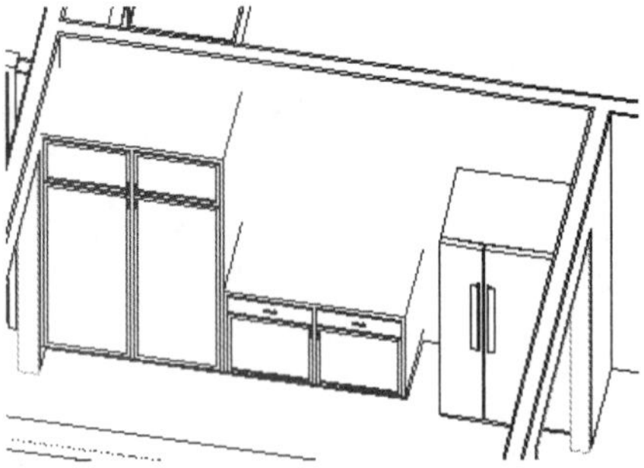

Add a refrigerator and additional cabinets to the other side of the kitchen.

7. 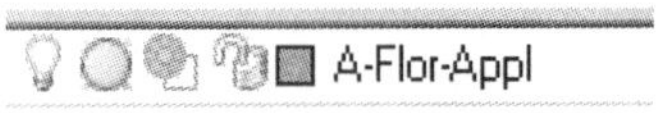


Select the refrigerator and the stove.
Note that these are placed on the *A-Flor-Appl* layer.

8. 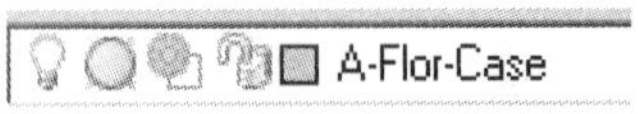


Select the cabinetry.
Note that these are placed on the *A-Flor-Case* layer.

9. 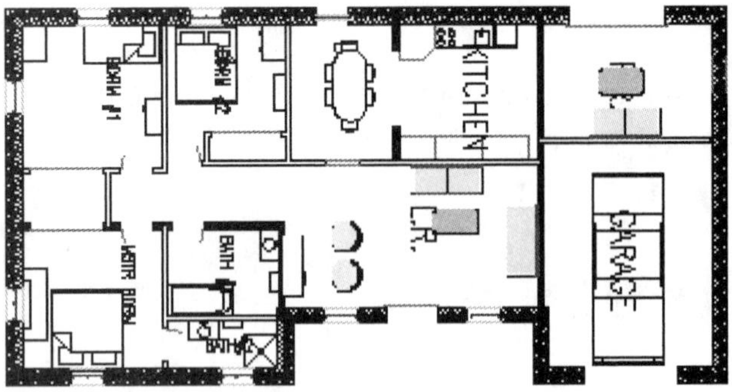


Our completed floor plan.

*The image is rotated 90 degrees.*

Save the file as *ex4-5.dwg*.

## Lesson 5
# Roofs

Roofs can be created with single or double slopes, with or without gable ends, and with or without overhangs. Once you input all your roof settings, you simply pick the points around the perimeter of the building to define your roof outline. If you make an error, you can easily modify or redefine your roof.

You need to pick three points before the roof will begin to preview in your graphics window. There is no limit to the number of points to select to define the perimeter.

To create a gable roof, uncheck the gable box in the Roof dialog. Pick the two end points for the sloped portion of the roof. Turn on the Gable box. Pick the end point for the gable side. Turn off the Gable box. Pick the end point for the sloped side. Turn the Gable box on. Pick the viewport and then press ENTER. A Gable cannot be defined with more than three consecutive edges.

Roofs can be created using two methods: ROOFADD places a roof based on points selected or ROOFCONVERT which converts a closed polyline or closed walls to develop a roof.

**TIP:** If you opt to use ROOFCONVERT and use existing closed walls, be sure that the walls are intersecting properly. If your walls are not properly cleaned up with each other, the roof conversion is unpredictable.

**TIP:** The Plate Height of a roof should be set equal to the Wall Height.

| | | |
|---|---|---|
| Shape –<br>Select the Shape option on the command line by typing 'S.' | Single Slope –<br>Extends a roof plane at an angle from the Plate Height. | <br>end elevation view |
| | Double Slope –<br>Includes a single slope and adds another slope, which begins at the intersection of the first slope and the height specified for the first slope. | <br>end elevation view |
| Gable –<br>Select the Gable option on the command line by typing 'G.' | If this is enabled, turns off the slope of the roof place. To create a gable edge, select Gable prior to identifying the first corner of the gable end. Turn off gable to continue to create the roof. | <br>gable roof end |
| Plate Height –<br>Set the Plate Height on the command line by typing 'PH.' | Specify the top plate from which the roof plane is projected. The height is relative to the XY plane with a Z coordinate of 0. | |
| Rise –<br>Set the Rise on the command line by typing 'PR.' | Sets the angle of the roof based on a run value of 12. | A rise value of 5 creates a 5/12 roof, which forms a slope angle of 22.62 degrees. |
| Slope –<br>Set the Slope on the command line by typing 'PS.' | Angle of the roof rise from the horizontal. | If slope angles are entered, then the rise will automatically be calculated. |
| Upper Height –<br>Set the Upper Height on the command line by typing 'UH.' | This is only available if a Double Slope roof is being created. This is the height where the second slope will start. | |

| | | |
|---|---|---|
| Rise (upper) – Set the Upper Rise on the command line by typing 'UR.' | This is only available if a Double Slope roof is being created. This is the slope angle for the second slope. | A rise value of 5 creates a 5/12 roof, which forms a slope angle of 22.62 degrees. |
| Slope (upper) – Set the Upper Slope on the command line by typing 'US.' | This is only available if a Double Slope roof is being created. Defines the slope angle for the second slope. | If an upper rise value is set, this is automatically calculated. |
| Overhang – To enable on the command line, type 'O.' To set the value of the Overhang, type 'V.' | If enabled, extends the roofline down from the plate height by the value set. | |

| | |
|---|---|
| | The Floating Viewer opens a viewer window displaying a preview of the roof. |
| | The match button allows you to select an existing roof to match its properties. |
| | The properties button opens the Roof Properties dialog. |
| | The Undo button allows you to undo the last roof operation. You can step back as many operations as you like up to the start. |
| | Opens the Roof Help file. |

**TIP:** You can create a gable on a roof by gripping any ridgeline point and stretching it past the roof edge. You cannot make a gable into a hip using grips.

# *Creating a Roof using Existing Walls*

Drawing Name:       ex3-1.dwg
Estimated Time:     15 minutes

This exercise reinforces the following skills:

    ❑   Convert to Roof

1.     Open *ex3-1.dwg.*

     Select the Work tab.
     Activate the right viewport that shows the top view.

2.     Launch the Tool Palette.

3.     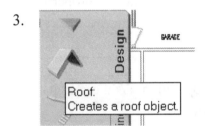    Select the Design tab.
                               Select the Roof tool.

4.     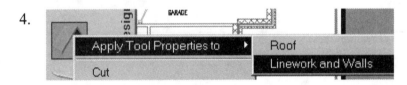    Right click and select
                                           **Apply Tool Properties
                                          to→Linework and Walls**.

5.     Select all the exterior walls in the drawing. Take care not to select any of the walls making up the chimney.
     Press Enter to continue.
     Enter **NO** to retain the layout geometry.

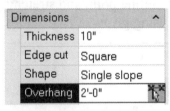    Expand the Dimensions section.
                               Set the Thickness to **10″**.
                               Set the Shape to **Single slope**.
                               Set the Overhang to **2′-0″**.

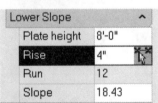    Expand the Lower Slope section.
                               Set the Plate height to **8′-0″**.
                               Set the Rise to **4″**.

6.

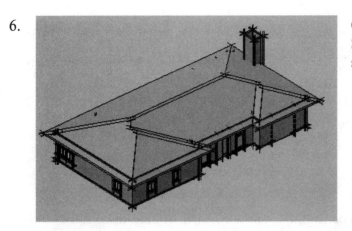

Close the Properties dialog.
Switch to paper space so you can
see your roof in both viewports.

7.   Save as *ex5-1.dwg*.

**Exercise 5-2:**
# Roof Slabs

Drawing Name:        ex5-1.dwg
Estimated Time:      15 minutes

This exercise reinforces the following skills:

- ❑  Convert to Roof
- ❑  Roof Slab Tools

Our roof works, but strictly speaking we can make it better with a couple of changes
around the chimney.  AutoCAD Architecture allows us to cut holes through roofs (to
allow for vents, chimneys and skylights), and to add other faces or subsidiary roofs such
as dormers.

In order to edit a roof you have to convert it to Roof Slabs.

1.        Open *ex5-1.dwg*.

Select the Work tab.
Activate the left viewport that shows the isometric view.

2.   AEC Modify Tools          Select the roof.

     Convert to Roof Slabs     Right click and select **Convert to Roof Slabs**.

     Edit Edges/Faces...

3.

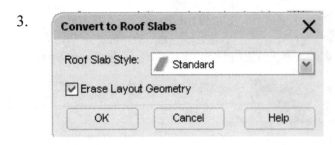

Enable the 'Erase layout geometry checkbox.

Press **OK**.

The Roof Slab Properties dialog appears.
Close it.

4.

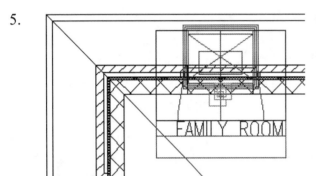

The roof will change appearance slightly. It now consists of individual slabs on the A-Roof-Slab layer.

5.

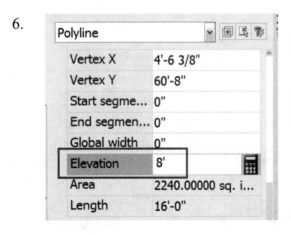

Activate the right viewport.
Zoom into the area where the chimney is located.

Draw a rectangle over the outline of the chimney. Make sure that the rectangle extends beyond the roof line.

6.

| Polyline | |
| --- | --- |
| Vertex X | 4'-6 3/8" |
| Vertex Y | 60'-8" |
| Start segme... | 0" |
| End segmen... | 0" |
| Global width | 0" |
| Elevation | 8' |
| Area | 2240.00000 sq. i... |
| Length | 16'-0" |

Select the rectangle.
Right click and select **Properties**.
Set the Elevation to **8'-0"**.

Close the Properties dialog.
Deselect the rectangle.

7.

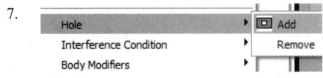

Select the roof slab located on top of the chimney.
Right click and select **Hole→Add**.

8. At the next prompt pick the rectangle. Be careful where you pick so you don't pick walls or furniture, which you can't see below the roof.
At the 'Erase Layout Geometry?' prompt hit, right click and select **Yes**.

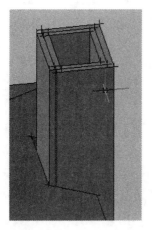

The hole will appear.

The chimney now appears OK.

Our roof as it exists has one problem at the chimney. The 'uphill' side of the chimney will catch water and snow. It needs a tiny little roof gable, called a cricket, to divert water away from the chimney. This will be done in the next exercise.

9.    Save as *ex5-2.dwg*.

### Exercise 5-3:
## Creating a Roof Cricket

Drawing Name:       ex5-2.dwg
Estimated Time:     10 minutes

This exercise reinforces the following skills:

- ❑  Layer User Groups
- ❑  Make Layer Current
- ❑  Isolate Layer Group

1.    Open *ex5-2.dwg*.

2.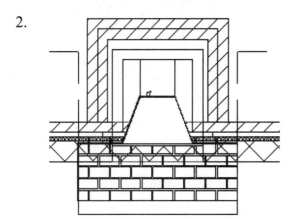

Select the plan view of the model.

Draw a rectangle 5'3-1/2" wide by 3' long, using the SE corner of the roof hole as the start point and going away from the hole.

You can use the wall edges of the chimney hole to guide you in the placement of the rectangle.

3. 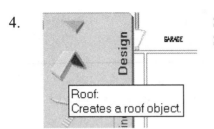 Launch the Tool Palette.

4. Select the Design tab.
Select the Roof tool.

5.  Right click and select
**Apply Tool Properties
to→Linework and Walls**.

6. 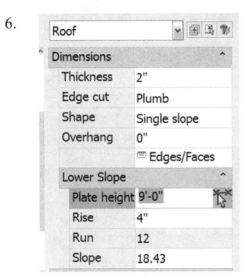 Pick the polyline (you can type 'l' for 'last' at the Select Objects prompt) and hit enter. Right click and select **No** for the 'Erase layout geometry?' prompt.

Sett the Thickness to **2″**.
Set the Edge cut to **Plumb**.
Set the Overhang to **0″**.
Set the plate height to **9′-0″**.
Make the rise **4″**.
Close the Properties dialog.

7. 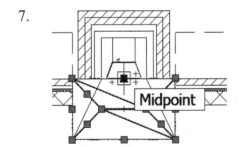 The new roof is hipped. Grip edit its ridge to make the exposed face a gable.
Pick the vertex of the triangle and stretch so it is aligned with the top horizontal line to create the gable.

8. 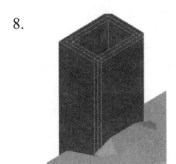 Here's a realistic shaded view from the other direction.

Save as *ex5-3.dwg*.

# QUIZ 3

## *True or False*

1. Custom content can be located in any subdirectory and still function properly.

2. The sole purpose of the Space Planning process is to arrange furniture in a floor plan.

3. The Design Center only has 3D objects stored in the Content area because AutoCAD Architecture is strictly a 3D software.

4. Appliances are automatically placed on the APPLIANCE layer.

5. When you place a wall cabinet, it is automatically placed at the specified height.

6. You can create tools on a tool palette by dragging and dropping the objects from the Design Center onto the palette.

## *Multiple Choice*

7. A residential structure is divided into:

    A. Four basic areas
    B. Three basic areas
    C. Two basic areas
    D. One basic area

8. Kitchen cabinets are located in the _____ subfolder.

    A. Casework
    B. Cabinets
    C. Bookcases
    D. Furniture

9. Select the area type that is NOT part of a private residence:

    A. Bedrooms
    B. Common Areas
    C. Service Areas
    D. Public Areas

10. To set the layer properties of a tool on a tool palette:

    A. Use the Layer Manager
    B. Select the tool, right click and select Properties.
    C. Launch the Properties dialog
    D. All of the above

11. Vehicles placed from the Design Center are automatically placed on this layer:

    A. A-Site-Vhcl
    B. A-Vhcl
    C. C-Site Vhcl
    D. None of the above

12. The **Roof** tool is located on this tool palette:

    A. DESIGN
    B. GENERAL DRAFTING
    C. MASSING
    D. TOOLS

**ANSWERS:**

1) T; 2) F; 3) F; 4) F; 5) T; 6) T; 7) B; 8) A; 9) D; 10) B; 11) C; 12) A

# Lesson 6
# Structural Members

Architectural documentation for residential construction will always include plans (top views) of each floor of a building, showing features and structural information of the floor platform itself. Walls are located on the plan but not shown in structural detail.

Wall sections and details are used to show:

- the elements within walls (exterior siding, sheathing, block, brick or wood studs, insulation, air cavities, interior sheathing, trim)
- how walls relate to floors, ceilings, roofs, eaves,
- openings within the walls (doors/windows with their associated sills and headers)
- how walls relate to openings in floors (stairs).

Stick-framed (stud) walls usually have their framing patterns determined by the carpenters on site. Once window and door openings are located on the plan, and stud spacing is specified by the designer (or the local building code), the specific arrangement of vertical members is usually left to the fabricators and not drafted, except where specific structural details require explanation.

The structural members in framed floors that have to hold themselves and/or other walls and floors up are usually drafted as framing plans. Designers must specify the size and spacing of joists or trusses, beams and columns. Plans show the orientation and relation of members, locate openings through the floor and show support information for openings and other specific conditions.

In the next exercises, we shall create a floor framing plan. Since the ground floor of our one-story lesson house has already been defined as a concrete slab, we'll assume that the ground level slopes down at the rear of the house and create a wood deck at the sliding door to the family room. The deck will need a railing for safety.

Autodesk AutoCAD Architecture includes a Structural Member Catalog that allows you to easily access industry-standard structural shapes. To create most standard column, brace, and beam styles, you can access the Structural Member Catalog, select a structural member shape, and create a style that contains the shape that you selected. The shape, similar to an AEC profile, is a 2D cross-section of a structural member. When you create a structural member with a style that you created from the Structural Member Catalog, you define the path to extrude the shape along.

You can create your own structural shapes that you can add to existing structural members, or use to create new structural members. The design rules in a structural member style allow you to add these custom shapes to a structural member, as well as create custom structural members from more than one shape.

All the columns, braces, and beams that you create are sub-types of a single Structural Member object type. The styles that you create for columns, braces, and beams have the same Structural Member Styles style type as well. When you change the display or style of a structural member, use the Structural Member object in the Display Manager and the Structural Member Styles style type in the Style Manager.

If you are operating with the AIA layering system as your current layer standard, when you create members or convert AutoCAD entities to structural members using the menu picks or toolbars, AutoCAD Architecture assigns the new members to layers: A-Cols, A-Cols-Brce or A-Beam, respectively. If Generic AutoCAD Architecture is your standard, the layers used are A_Columns, A_Beams and A_Braces. If your layer standard is Current Layer, new entities come in on the current layer, as in plain vanilla AutoCAD.

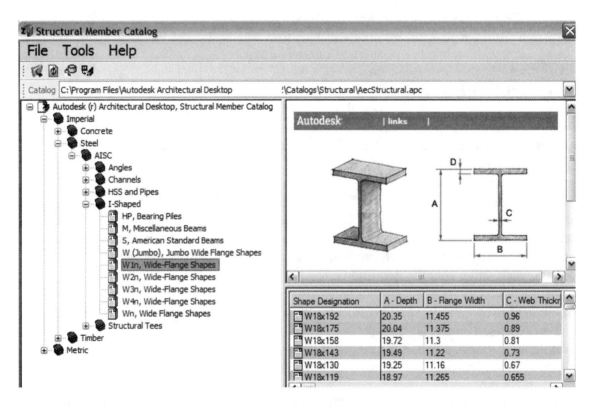

The Structural Member Catalog includes specifications for standard structural shapes. You can choose shapes from the Structural Member Catalog, and generate styles for structural members that you create in your drawings.

The left pane of the Structural Member Catalog contains a hierarchical tree view. Several industry standard catalogs are organized in the tree, first by imperial or metric units, and then by material.

| | |
|---|---|
| | Open a catalog file - The default is the catalog that comes with AutoCAD Architecture, but you can create your own custom catalog. The default catalog is located in the following directory path:  \\Program Files\Autodesk AutoCAD Architecture R3\Catalogs\catalogs. |
| | Refresh Data |
| | Locate Catalog item based on an existing member – allows you to select a member in a drawing and then locates it in your catalog. |
| | Generate Member Style – allows you to create a style to be used. |

We will be adding a wood framed deck, 14′ x 9′, to the back of the house. For purposes of this exercise we will assume that the ground level is 12″ below the slab at the back of the house and falls away so that grade level below the edge of the deck away from the house is 6′ below floor level: -6′-0″ a.f.f. (above finish floor) in architectural notation. We will place the top of the deck floorboards even with the top of the floor slab.

We will use support and rim joists as in standard wood floor framing, and they will all be at the same level, rather than joists crossing a support beam below. In practice this means the use of metal hangers, which will not be drawn. Once the floor system is drawn we will add support columns at the outside rim joist and braces at the columns.

### Exercise 6-1:
## Creating Member Styles

Drawing Name:     ex5-3.dwg
Estimated Time:    15 minutes

This exercise reinforces the following skills:

- ❑  Creating Member Styles
- ❑  Use of Structural Members tools

1.    Open *ex5-3.dwg.*
Select the Work tab.
Activate the right viewport.

2.    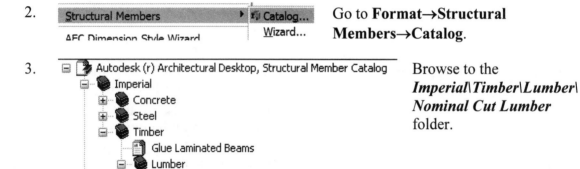    Go to **Format→Structural Members→Catalog**.

3.    Browse to the *Imperial\Timber\Lumber\ Nominal Cut Lumber* folder.

4.    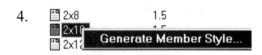    Locate the **2x10** shape designation.
Right click and select **Generate Member Style**.

5.    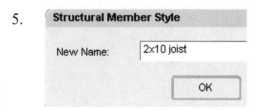    In the Structural Member Style dialog box, type **2x10 joist** – the name for your style.

Click **OK**.

A style that contains the catalog shape that you selected is created. You can view the style in the Style Manager, create a new structural member from the style, or apply the style to an existing member.

When you add a structural member to your drawing, the shape inside the style that you created defines the shape of the member. You define the length, justification, roll or rise, and start and end offsets of the structural member when you draw it.

You cannot use the following special characters in your style names:

- less-than and greater-than symbols (< >)
- forward slashes and backslashes (/ \)
- quotation marks (")
- colons (:)
- semicolons (;)
- question marks (?)
- commas (,)
- asterisks (*)
- vertical bars (|)
- equal signs (=)
- backquotes (`)

6. 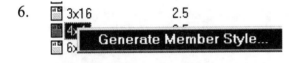   Locate the **4x4** Shape Designation.
Right click and select **Generate Member Style**.

7. 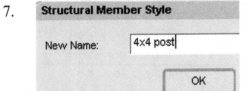   Type **4x4 post** in the New Name field.
Press **OK**.

8. 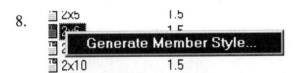   Select the **2x6** Shape Designation.
Right click and select **Generate Member Style**.

9. 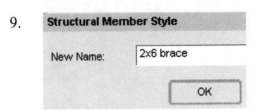   Type **2x6 brace** in the New Name field.
Close the catalog.

10.   Launch the Tool Palette.

11.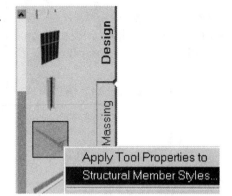

Select the Design tab.

Select the Structural Beam tool.
Right click and select **Structural Member Styles**.

12.

Under Architectural Objects, expand the Structural Member Styles.

```
☐ ⊞ ex5-3.dwg
  ☐ ☐ Architectural Objects
    ☐ ▌ Structural Member Styles
      ┃ ▌ 2x10 joist
      ┃ ▌ 2x6 brace
      ┃ ▌ 4x4 post
      └ ▌ Standard
```

We see the styles we just created.

Close the Style Manager dialog.

13. Save as *ex6-1.dwg*.

## Exercise 6-2:
## *Adding Structural Members*

Drawing Name:       ex6-1.dwg
Estimated Time:     25 minutes

This exercise reinforces the following skills:

 ❑ Creating Member Styles
 ❑ Use of Structural Members tools

1.     Open *ex6-1.dwg*.

Select the Work tab.
Activate the right viewport.

2.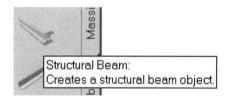

Select the Structural Beam tool on the Design Palette.

3.

| BASIC | ⌃ |
| --- | --- |
| **General** | ⌃ |
| Description | 🔲 |
| Style | ‖ Standard ⌄ |
| Bound spaces | ‖ 2x10 joist |
| Trim autom... | ‖ 2x6 brace |
| Member type | ‖ 4x4 post |

Select the 2x10 joist from the Style drop-down.

4.

| A | Start of... | 0" |
| --- | --- | --- |
| B | End off... | 0" |
| C | Logica... | 2" |
| E | Roll | 0.00 |
| | Justify | Top Right |
| | Justify ... | Yes |

Set Justify to **Top Right**.
Set the Roll to **0**.
Set the Start Offset to **0″**.

5. Zoom into the family room area (the top left of the floor plan).

Use the From OSNAP, pick the upper left corner of the house wall, and type '@1.5<-90' for the Offset; press ENTER. This shifts the first beam slightly below the wall.

Pull the cursor down at a 270° angle, and type in 13'-9″ for the length.
DO NOT EXIT THE COMMAND.

```
Command: _AecsBeamAdd
Start point or [STyle/STArt offset/ENd offset/Justify/Roll/Match]: _from Base
point: <Offset>: @1.5<-90

End point or [STyle/STArt offset/ENd offset/Justify/Roll/Match]: 13'-9"

End point or [STyle/STArt offset/ENd offset/Justify/Roll/Match/Undo]:
```

6. Change the Justification to Top Left.
Pull the cursor to the left (180°) and enter 9' for the length.

Hit enter to terminate the command.

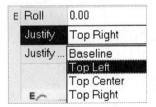

| E | Roll | 0.00 |
| --- | --- | --- |
| | Justify | Top Right |
| | Justify ... | Baseline |
| | | Top Left |
| | | Top Center |
| E⌒ | | Top Right |

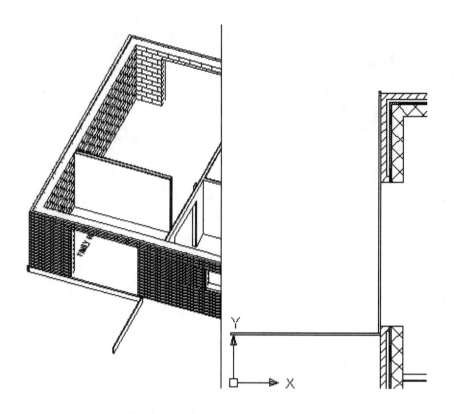

---

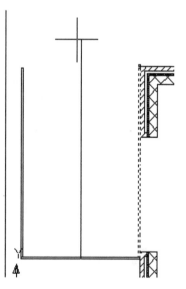

**TIP:** If you have difficulty starting the beam, draw the first two beams to the left of the building and then move them into position.

7.  Mirror the first joist. (Use the Midpoint OSNAP with Polar or Ortho.)

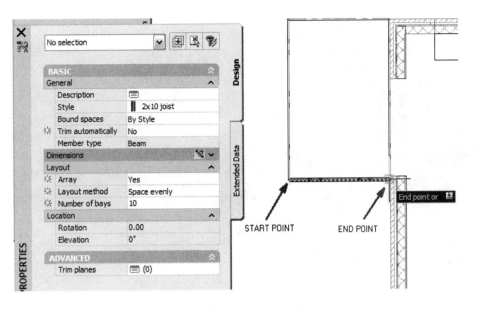

8. Select the **Structural Beam** tool on the Design Palette.

9. Set the Style to **2x10 joist**.
   Under Layout: Set Array to **Yes**.
   Set Layout Method to **Space evenly**.
   Set Number of bays to **10**.

10. Select the start and end points indicated.
    You should see a preview image of the array that will be placed.

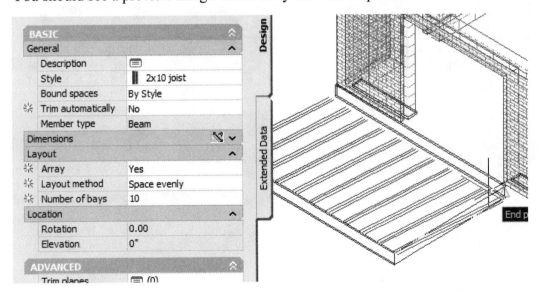

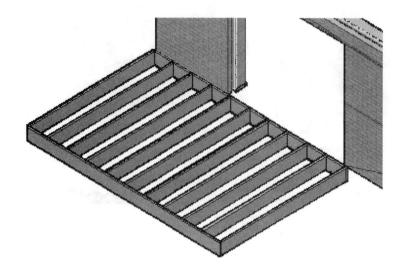

The array is placed.

## Adding Columns

11.

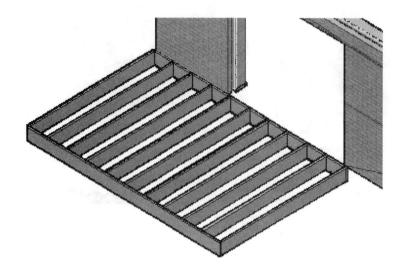

Select the **Structural Column** tool from the Design Palette.

12. Set the Style to **4x4 post**.
Set the Length to **6'-0"**.
Set Justify to **Bottom Left**.
Set the Roll to **0**.

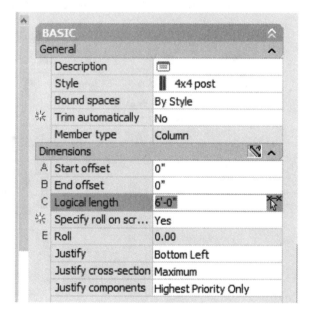

13.

In the right viewport, use the From OSNAP, pick the lower left corner of the joist frame, and enter '@0,24,-6'-0''' to place the post so the left face aligns with the outside of the doubled joist, the bottom face is 2' from the bottom edge, and the top is even with the bottom of the joists.

14. Mirror the post to place another column 2' in from the top (left side) of the frame.

15. Zoom in to the isometric view of the structure.

16.

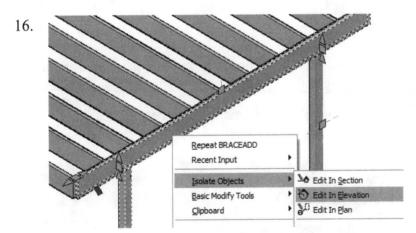

Select the front joist and the two posts. You may select using crossing, window, the control key, and de-select using the shift key.

Right click and select **Isolate Objects→Edit In Elevation**.

This will temporarily hide all the objects that were not selected and switch the display to an elevation view.

17. Select the front of the horizontal joist when prompted to select a face to use as a reference for the elevation.

## Adding Braces

18.

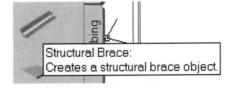

Select the **Structural Brace** tool from the Design Palette.

19.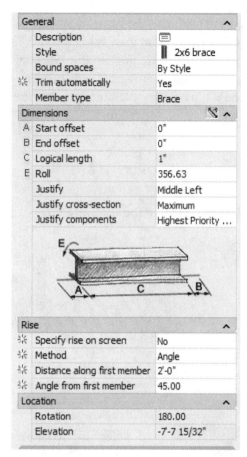

Set the Style to **2x6 brace**.
Set the Roll to **0**.
Set Specify rise on Screen to **No**.
Set the Distance along first member to **2'-0"**.
Set Justify to **Middle Left**.
Set the Method to **Angle**.

20.

Select the mid-point of the post and then the front face of the joist.

The brace will automatically place and trim itself.

21.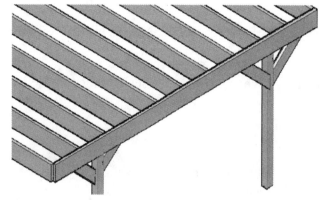

Use the Structural Brace tool to place a brace on the other post.

Use Mirror to copy the brace to the other side of each post.

22. Save as *ex6-2.dwg*.

*Exercise 6-3:*
## Miter Corners

Drawing Name:     ex6-2.dwg
Estimated Time:   15 minutes

This exercise reinforces the following skills:

- ❑ Structural Members
- ❑ Use of Structural Members tools

The Miter tool was new to ADT 2007.

1. Open *ex6-2.dwg*.

2. Zoom into a corner of the decking.

3. Select one of the beams.
   Right click and select
   **Trim Planes→Miter**.

4. Select the adjacent beam to miter.

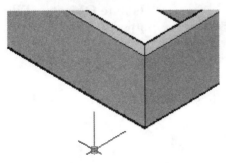

   The corner is perfectly trimmed.

5. Repeat for the other three corners of the deck.

6. Save as *ex6-3.dwg*.

### Exercise 6-4:
## Add Floorboards

Drawing Name:     ex6-3.dwg
Estimated Time:   20 minutes

This exercise reinforces the following skills:

- ❑ Structural Members
- ❑ Use of Structural Members tools

The top of the joist frame we created in the last exercise is sitting even with the top of the floor slab. It needs to be lowered to allow for nominal 2x6 deck boards.

1.   Open *ex6-3.dwg*.

   Select the Work tab.
   Activate the right viewport.

2.   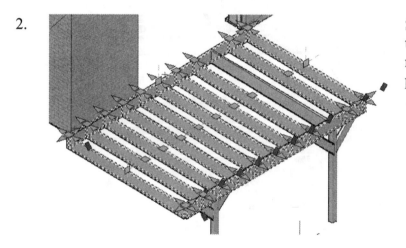 Select the joists that form the base of the deck. Do not select the braces or the posts.

3.   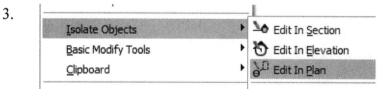 Right click and select **Isolate Objects→Edit In Plan**.

4.   Select a top face of one of the joists to switch to a plan view.

5.   Select the **Structural Beam** tool.

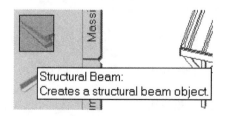

6.

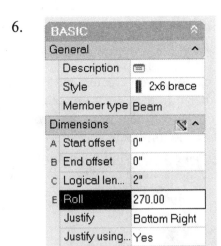

Set the Style to **2x6 brace**.

Set the Roll to **270°**, so that it lies flat rather than vertical.

Set the Justification to **Bottom Right**, so the board sits on top of the joists.

7.

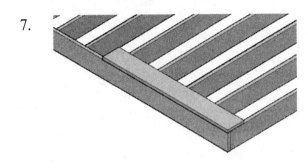

Pick the lower right corner of the joist at the house wall, drag the cursor up (90°), and give the board a length of 8'. Drag the cursor up at 90° and add a second board of length 6'.

---

**TIP:** If you have difficulty starting the beam, draw the first beam to the left of the building and then move it into position.

8.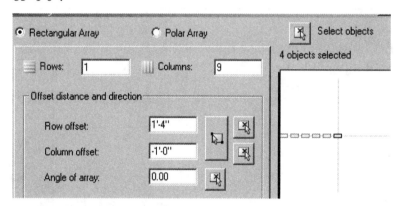

Enter twice to terminate and restart the command so you can pick a new starting point.

Pick the lower left corner of the first deck board you created, pull the cursor up at 90°, enter a distance of 4′, then pull the cursor up at 90° and enter a distance of 10′.  (Although not strictly necessary, we are providing suggested lengths of deck boards to minimize wastage.) Deck boards are laid with a nominal ½″ space between them to allow for drainage and board warping, so move the last two deck boards ½″ to the left.

9. Array the 4 deck boards to fill the deck: 1 row, 9 columns with a column offset of -1′0″.

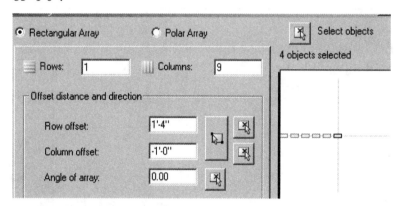

10.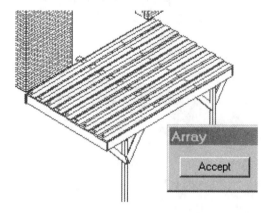

Use the Preview option of the Array to check your array.

Press **Accept**.

11. 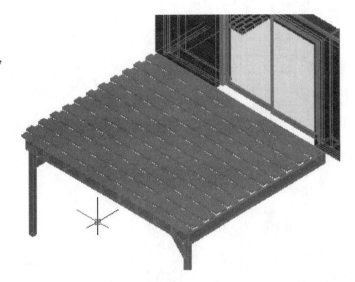 Select the **Exit Edit In View** button.

*Note: You want a gap between the boards to allow for expansion and compression due to seasonal changes.*

12. Save as *ex6-4.dwg*.

### Exercise 6-5:
## Add Railing

Drawing Name:     Ex6-4.dwg
Estimated Time:   15 minutes

This exercise reinforces the following skills:

❑ Railings
❑ Railing Styles

Next, we create a railing for the deck.

1.  Open *ex6-4.dwg*.

Select the Work tab.
Activate the right viewport.

2. 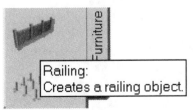 Select the **Railing** tool from the Design Palette.

3.

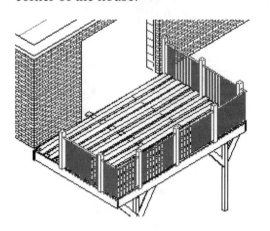

Pick the lower right corner of the deck for the start point.

Create endpoints at 9' to the left (180°), then 14' up (90°), and 6' to the right (0°). This leaves a 3' opening at the corner of the house.

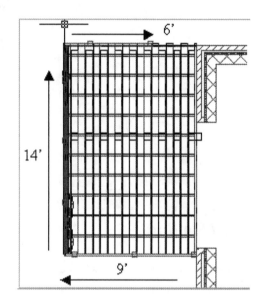

## Railing Styles

4.

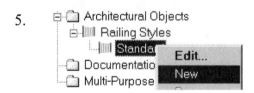

Select the **Railing** tool from the Design Palette. Right click and select **Railing Styles**.

5. Select **Standard** under Railing Styles. Right click and select **New**.

6. Select the **New Style**. Right click and select **Rename**.

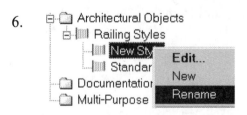

7.   ⊟ Railing Styles     Name the new railing style **Deck**.
         Deck
         Standard

8.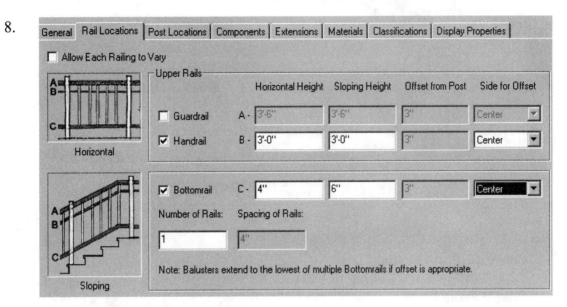

Select the **Rail Locations** tab.
Enable **Handrail** for the Upper Rails.
Set the Horizontal Height to **3'**.
Set the Sloping Height to **3'**.
Set the Side for Offset to **Center**.
Enable the **Bottom Rail**.  (This adds a bottom rail)
Set the Horizontal Height to **4"**.
Set the Sloping Height to **6"**.
Set the Number of Rails to **1**.

9.

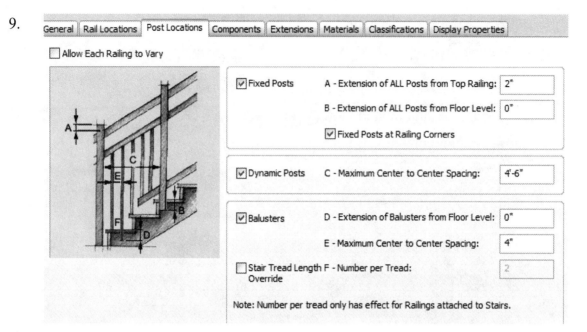

Select the **Post Locations** tab.
Disable **Allow Each Railing to Vary**.
Enable **Fixed Posts**.
Enable **Fixed Posts at Railing Corners**. (This adds a post to each corner)
Set the Extensions of ALL Posts from Top Railing to **2″**.
Enable **Dynamic Posts**.
Set the Maximum Center to Center Spacing to **4′-6″**.
Enable **Balusters**.
Set the Maximum Center to Center Spacing to **4″**.
Disable the **Stair Tread Length Override**.

10. Select the **Components** tab.
Change the Width of the Guardrail to **3″**.
All the other settings are unchanged.

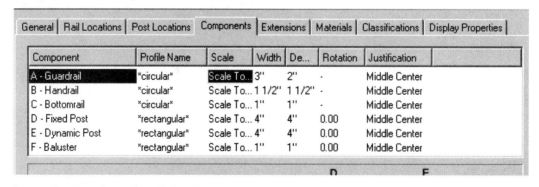

Press **OK** to close the dialog box.

Press **Apply** and **OK**.

## Changing a Railing Style

11.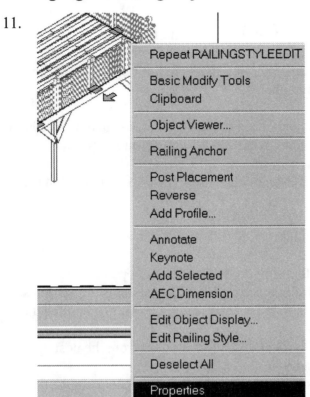

Select the Railing.
Right click and select **Properties**.

12.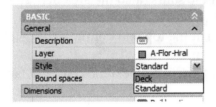

Change the Style to **Deck**.
Close the dialog.

13. Save as *ex6-5.dwg*.

## *Stairs*

A house may have main stairs (from the first floor to the second floor) and/or a set of service stairs. Main stairs are usually constructed using pre-fabricated parts and are generally of better quality than service stairs. Service stairs are built on location. They are generally constructed of construction lumber.

There are six general types of stairs commonly used in residential construction. They are straight-run, L stairs, double-L stairs, U stairs, winder stairs and spiral stairs.

Straight run stairs are the most common. They are the least expensive to build, but they require a long open space.

Common terms associated with stairs include:

| | |
|---|---|
| Balusters: | vertical members that support the handrail on open stairs |
| Enclosed stairs: | stairs that have a wall on both sides (also known as closed, housed, or box stairs). These can be stairs leading down to a basement or cellar. |
| Headroom: | The shortest clear vertical distance measured from the nosing of the tread and the ceiling. |
| Housed stringer: | A stringer that has been routed or grooved to accommodate the treads and risers. |
| Landing: | The floor area at either end of the stairs; also the area between a set of stairs, such as in an L stairs. |
| Newel: | The main posts of the handrail at the top and bottom or at points where the stairs change direction. |
| Nosing: | The rounded projection of the tread which extends past the face of the riser. |

We will be adding service stairs to our deck.

*Exercise 6-6:*
## Add Stairs

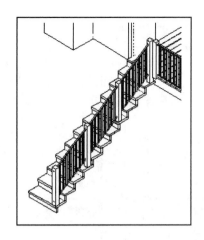

Drawing Name:    Ex6-5.dwg
Estimated Time:    15 minutes

This exercise reinforces the following skills:

- □  Add Stairs
- □  Add Railing

1.    Open *ex6-5.dwg*.

Select the Work tab.
Activate the right viewport.

2.    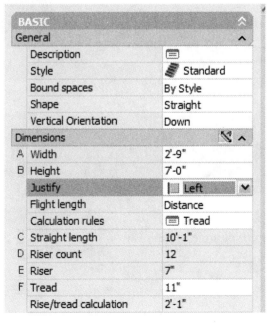    Select the **Stair** tool from the Design Palette.

Stair:
Creates a stair object.

3.

| BASIC | |
|---|---|
| General | |
| Description | |
| Style | Standard |
| Bound spaces | By Style |
| Shape | Straight |
| Vertical Orientation | Down |
| Dimensions | |
| A  Width | 2'-9" |
| B  Height | 7'-0" |
| Justify | Left |
| Flight length | Distance |
| Calculation rules | Tread |
| C  Straight length | 10'-1" |
| D  Riser count | 12 |
| E  Riser | 7" |
| F  Tread | 11" |
| Rise/tread calculation | 2'-1" |

Set the Style to **Standard**.
Set the Shape to **Straight**.
Set the Vertical Orientation to **Down**.
Set the Width to **2'-9"**.
Set the Height to **7'**.
Set the Tread to **11"**.
Set Justify to **Left**.

Note that the Straight length is
automatically calculated at 10'-1".

4. 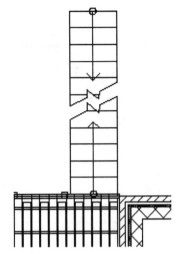 Pick an end point by the left side of the deck opening near the start of the railing.

Pick a point near the top of the deck for the end point of the stairs.

Close the dialog box.

## Stair Representation

5. We see the stair as a broken view because of the Options setting in our AEC Stair Defaults.

Bring up the **Options** Dialog box.

6. 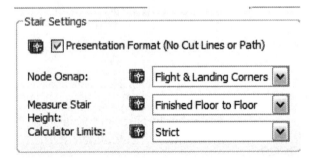 Place your cursor in the command line.
Right click and select **Options**.

7. Select the **AEC Object Settings** tab.
Enable the Presentation Format.

8.

Stair Settings

☑ Presentation Format (No Cut Lines or Path)

Node Osnap: Flight & Landing Corners

Measure Stair Height: Finished Floor to Floor

Calculator Limits: Strict

Press **Apply** and **OK**.
Notice that the stairs appearance does not change.

9.  Type **Regen**.
    The stairs now appear without a break mark.

    *Note: If the view doesn't update, try switching to a different view and then switch back to Plan view.*

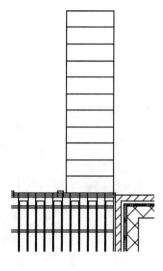

10.  The stairs are placed, but they may need to be shifted slightly to fit with the deck.
    Use the **Move** tool to position the stairs properly.
    Safety regulations require a handrail down the stairs.

## Add Railing

11.  Select the **Railing** tool from the Design Palette.

12. 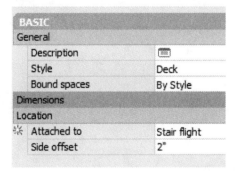 Set the Style to **Deck**.
    Set Attached to: **Stair Flight**.
    Set Offset to **2"**.

13. 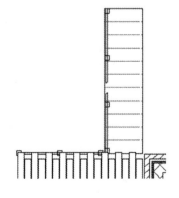 You will be prompted to select the stairs.
    Pick the left side of the stair to place railing on the left side.

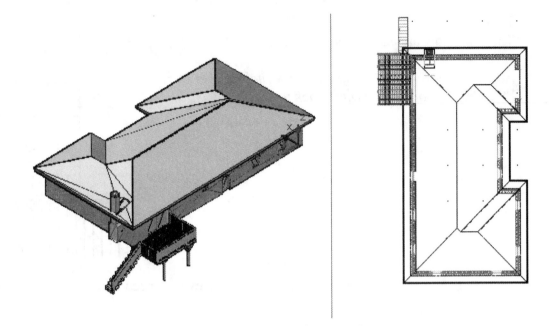

14.   Save as *ex6-6.dwg.*

## Lesson 7
# Layouts

Before we can create our construction drawings, we need to create layouts or views to present the design. AutoCAD Architecture is similar to AutoCAD in that the user can work in Model and Paper Space. Model Space is where we create the 3D model of our house. Paper Space is where we create or setup various views that can be used in our construction drawings. In each view, we can control what we see by turning off layers, zooming, panning, etc.

To understand paper space and model space, imagine a cardboard box. Inside the cardboard box is Model Space. This is where your 3D model is located. On each side of the cardboard box, tear out a small rectangular window. The windows are your viewports. You can look through the viewports to see your model. To reach inside the window so you can move your model around or modify it, you double-click inside the viewport. If your hand is not reaching through any of the windows and you are just looking from the outside, then you are in Paper Space.

You can create an elevation in your current drawing by first drawing an elevation line and mark, and then creating a 2D or 3D elevation based on that line. You can control the size and shape of the elevation that is generated. Unless you explode the elevation that you create, the elevation remains linked to the building model that you used to create it. Because of this link between the elevation and the building model, any changes to the building model can be made in the elevation as well.

When you create a 2D elevation, the elevation is created with hidden and overlapping lines removed. You can edit the 2D elevation that you created by changing its display properties. The 2D Section/Elevation style allows you to add your own display components to the display representation of the elevation, and create rules that assign different parts of the elevation to different display components. You can control the visibility, layer, color, linetype, lineweight, and linetype scale of each component. You can also use the line work editing commands to assign individual lines in your 2D elevation to display components, and merge geometry into your 2D elevation.

After you create a 2D elevation, you can use the AutoCAD BHATCH and AutoCAD DIMLINEAR commands to hatch and dimension the 2D elevation.

### Exercise 7-1:
## Creating a Custom Toolbar

Drawing Name:     NEW
Estimated Time:    20 minutes

This exercise reinforces the following skills:

- ❑ Toolbars
- ❑ Commands
- ❑ Customization
- ❑ Attributes

1.         Select the **QNEW** tool.

2. Right click in the gray area of a toolbar.
Select **Customize**.

*There will be a slight pause when the Customize User Interface Dialog loads.*

3. Highlight the Toolbars category.
Right click and select **New→Toolbar**.

4. 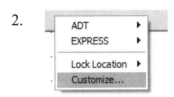 Change the name of the toolbar to **Block Tools**.

5. Select the **All Commands** category from the drop down list.

Locate the **Define Attributes** command.

6. Drag and drop the command into the Block Tools category.

You will see an arrow to indicate that you have placed the command in the correct location.

7. The command will be listed on the Block Tools list.

8. Select the **All Commands** category from the drop down list.

Locate the **Edit Attribute** tool.

9.  Block Tools
    Define Attributes...
    Menus

    Drag and drop the command into the Block Tools category.

    You will see a bar to indicate that you have placed the command in the correct location.

10. Block Tools
    Edit Attribute...
    Define Attributes...

    The command will be listed on the Block Tools list.

11. Press **Apply** and **OK** to close the Customize dialog.

      The new toolbar appears in your graphics window along with any other toolbars you added.

12. Close the drawing without saving.


## Exercise 7-2:
## *Creating an Elevation Label*

Drawing Name:     NEW
Estimated Time:   35 minutes

This exercise reinforces the following skills:

- Blocks
- Elevation Labels
- Create AEC Custom Content
- Attributes
- Workspaces

1.  Select the **QNEW** tool.

    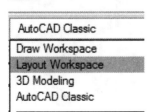

    Set the **Layout** workspace.

    This resets your user interface for the creation of documents.

2.  Launch the Design Center.

3.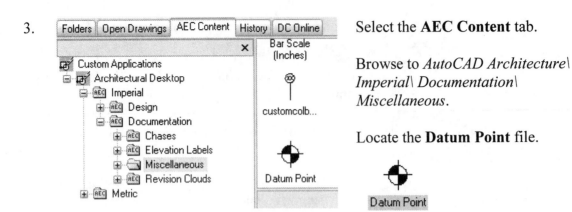

Select the **AEC Content** tab.

Browse to *AutoCAD Architecture\ Imperial\ Documentation\ Miscellaneous*.

Locate the **Datum Point** file.

4.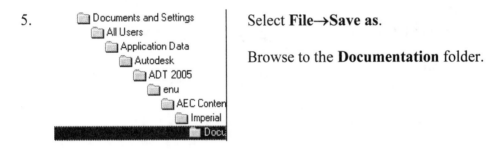

Select the Datum Point file.
Right click and select **Open**.

5.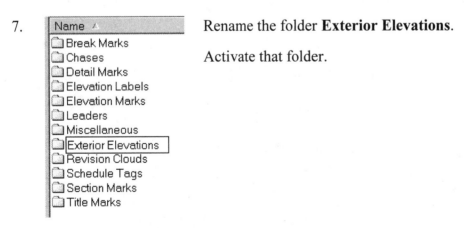

Select **File→Save as**.

Browse to the **Documentation** folder.

6. Select the **Create New Folder** tool.

7. 

Rename the folder **Exterior Elevations**.

Activate that folder.

Name ⌃
Break Marks
Chases
Detail Marks
Elevation Labels
Elevation Marks
Leaders
Miscellaneous
Exterior Elevations
Revision Clouds
Schedule Tags
Section Marks
Title Marks

8. 

File name: elevation level.dwg

Files of type: AutoCAD 2007 Drawing (*.dwg)

Name your file **elevation level**.
Press **Save**.

9. Draw a 6″ long horizontal line.

10. Add two attributes:
One for level and one for elevation.

11.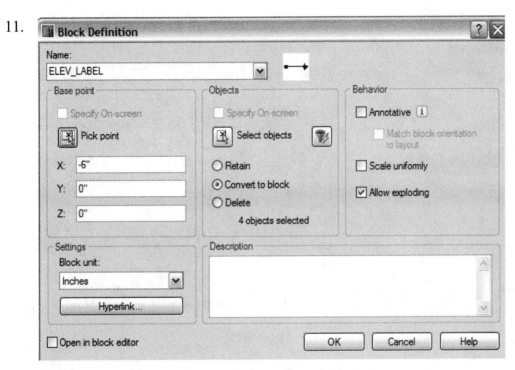

Select the **Make Block** tool.

In the Name field, enter **Elev_label**.

Select the objects in the drawings.

Select the end point of the horizontal line as the insertion point.

Select **Convert to Block**.

Enable **Allow exploding**.

Press **OK**.

12.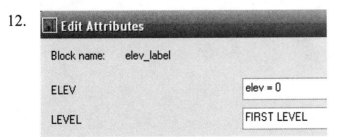

The Edit Attributes dialog will appear.

Fill in the attribute values.

Press **OK**.

13.   AEC Content Wizard...          Go to **Format→AEC Content Wizard**.
      Define Schedule Tag...

14.   Content Type                   Enable **Custom Command**.
      ○ Block
      ○ Drawing
      ○ Multi-View Block
      ○ Masking Block
      ◉ Custom Command

15.   Current Drawing:          Content File:     Select the **elev_label** block
      Anno_Datum                elev_label        using the Add tool and
      elev_label                                  remove any other blocks listed
                      Add >>>                      in the Content File window.
                      <<< Remove

16.   Command String:                In the Command String field enter
      _AecAnnoSymbolAdd _SYMBOL elev_label    **AecAnnoSymbolAdd SYMBOL elev_label.**

                                     Press **Next**.

17.   Place a check next to **Enable AEC Unit Scaling**.
      This automatically scales your block to the current viewport.
      The Layer Key assigns the layer to place your block.
      Press **Next**.

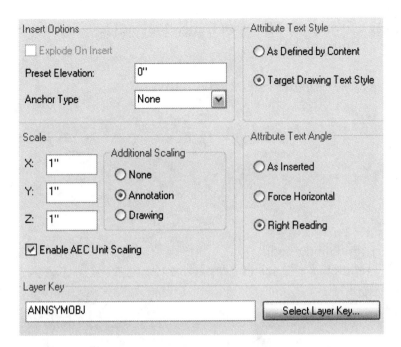

18. Enable **Current Drawing**.
    Press **Default Icon** to select the drawing's preview icon.

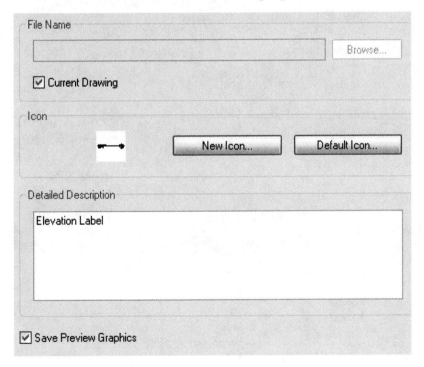

Press **Finish**.

19. Press **Save** and **Close**.

20. Right click in the Design Center Window and select **Refresh**.

21.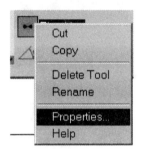

Drag and drop the **Elevation Label** from the Design Center onto the Annotation Palette.

Close the Design Center by typing **Ctl+2**.

22.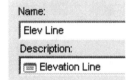

Highlight the tool.
Right click and select **Properties**.

23. 

Change the name to **Elev Line**.

Change the Description to **Elevation Line**.

24.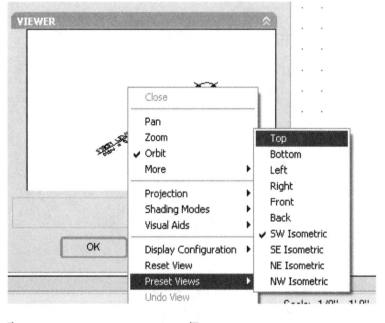

Scroll down to the Viewer window.

Right click and select **Preset Views→Top**.

25.

The view will update to the top view.

26. 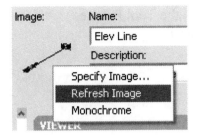 Right click on the Image icon.
Select **Refresh Image**.

27. Press **OK** and close the Properties dialog.

28. Drag and drop the block into your drawing.

You should be prompted for the attribute values.
The icon should be placed on the correct layer – A- ANNO SYMB.

29. Zoom Extents.

30. Type SAVEIMG on the command line.

Set the Format to **BMP** and press **OK**.

31. Locate a folder to store your file.
Name your image **elev.bmp**.

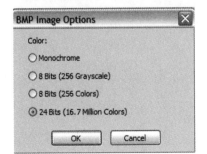

Enable **24 Bit**s.

Press **OK**.

32.   Select the **Elev Line** tool on the Tool Palette.
Right click and select Properties.

33. 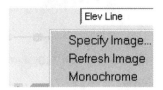  Place your cursor on the image.
Right click and select **Specify Image**.

34. 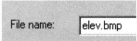  Locate the image you created.
Press **Open**.

35. Press OK to close the Properties dialog.

36. Close the drawing without saving.

*Exercise 7-3:*
# *Creating an Elevation Window Tag*

Drawing Name:      NEW
Estimated Time:    25 minutes

This exercise reinforces the following skills:

- ❑ Blocks
- ❑ Elevation Labels
- ❑ Create AEC Custom Content
- ❑ Attributes

1. Select the **QNEW** tool.

2. Select the **Polygon** tool.

   Set the number of sides to **6**.
   For the center point, enter **0,0,0**.
   Set the polygon to **Inscribed.**
   Set the Radius to **1/8"**.
   Use Zoom Extents to see the polygon you just created.

**TIP:** ADT only allows the user to specify a single path for Content. You can create a custom subdirectory under the Content path in order to protect your custom files.

3. Select the Define Attribute tool.

The tag should be set to **WINDOWOBJECTS:NUMBER**.
The prompt should be set to **WINDOW NO**.
The default value should be set to **000**.
The Insertion Point should be set to **0,0,0**.
Set the Text Height to **1/16″**.
Set the Justification to **Center**.
Press **OK**.

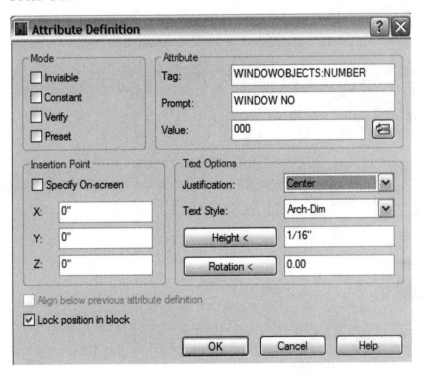

4. Select the Define Attribute tool.

The tag should be set to **WINDOWSTYLES:TYPE**.
The prompt should be set to **TYPE**.
The default value should be set to **STD**.
Ste the Mode to **Invisible**.
Enable Align below previous attribute definition.

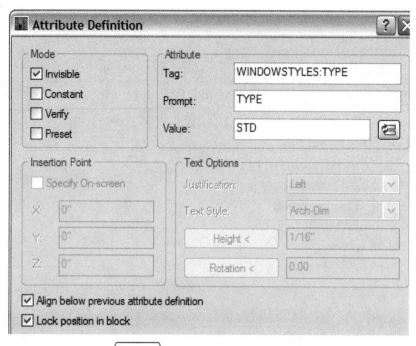

WINDOWOBJECTS:NUMBER
WINDOWSTYLES:TYPE

Press **OK**.

5.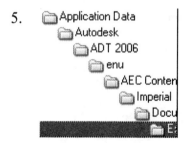

Verify that you are in the Exterior Elevation folder you created earlier.

6.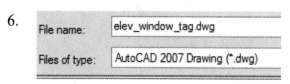

Select **Save**.
Enter **elev_window_tag** for the file name.

7.   Go to **Format→Style Manager**.

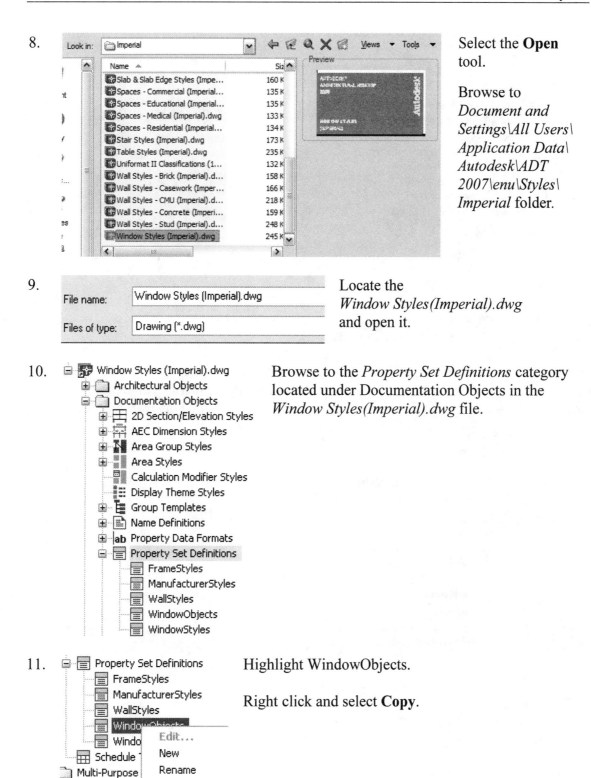

8.    Select the **Open** tool.

Browse to *Document and Settings\All Users\ Application Data\ Autodesk\ADT 2007\enu\Styles\ Imperial* folder.

9.    Locate the *Window Styles(Imperial).dwg* and open it.

10.   Browse to the *Property Set Definitions* category located under Documentation Objects in the *Window Styles(Imperial).dwg* file.

11.   Highlight WindowObjects.

Right click and select **Copy**.

12.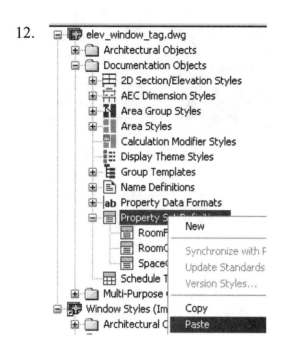

Locate the *Property Set Definitions* folder in the elev_window_tag.dwg file.

Right click and select **Paste**.

13.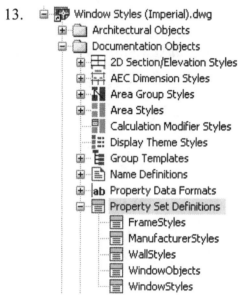

Browse to the *Property Set Definitions* category located under Documentation Objects in the *Window Styles(Imperial).dwg* file.

14. 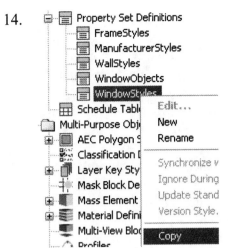 Highlight WindowStyles.

Right click and select **Copy**.

15.  Locate the *Property Set Definitions* folder in the elev_window_tag.dwg file.

Right click and select **Paste**.

16. Close the Style Manager dialog by pressing **Apply** and **OK**.

17. 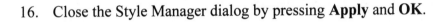 Select the **Make Block** tool or type **BLOCK** if the tool is not available.

18.

Enter the name *elev_window*.

Select the center point of the polygon as the base point.

Select the two attributes and the polygon.

Enable **Allow exploding**.

Enter a description.

Press **OK**.

19.

| Edit Attributes | |
|---|---|
| Block name: | elev_window |
| WINDOW NO | 000 |
| TYPE | STD |

The Edit Attributes dialog will appear.

Press **OK**.

20. Go to **Format→AEC Content Wizard**.

21.

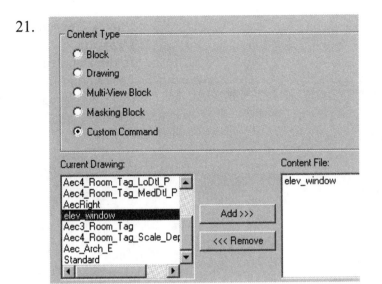

Enable **Custom Command**.

Highlight the *elev_window* block.

Press **Add**.

22.

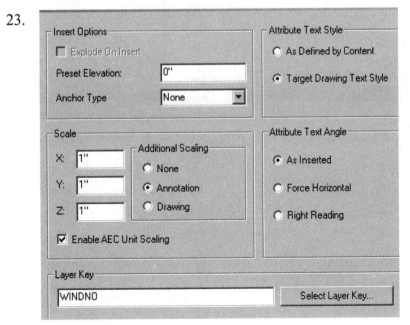

Define your custom command as shown.

Press **OK**.

Press **Next**.

23.

Enable **Enable AEC Unit Scaling**.

Set the Layer Key to **WINDNO**.

Press **Next**.

24.

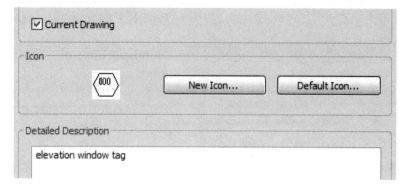

Enable **Current Drawing**.
In the Detailed Description field, enter **elevation window tag**.

Press **Finish**.

25.  Save as *elev_window_tag*.

Close the file.

*Exercise 7-4:*
## Creating a Custom Titleblock

Drawing Name:       Architectural Title Block.dwg
Estimated Time:     30 minutes

This exercise reinforces the following skills:

- ❑ Title blocks
- ❑ Attributes
- ❑ Layouts

1.  Select the **Open** tool.

2.

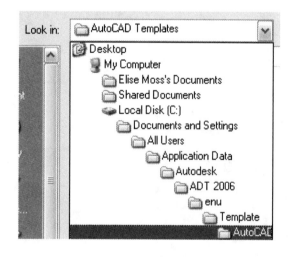

Browse to
*Documents and Settings\All Users\ Application Data\Autodesk\ADT 2007\ enu\ Template\AutoCAD Templates.*

3. 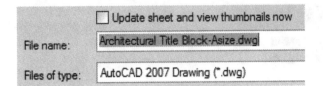 Open the *Architectural Title Block.dwg*

4. Perform a **File→Save as**.

   Save the file to your work folder.
   Rename **Architectural Title Block-Asize.dwg**.

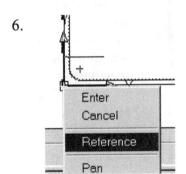

5. Select the **Scale** tool or type **SCALE**.

6. 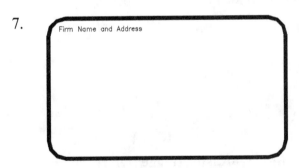 Type **ALL** to select the title block.
   Select the lower left point as the base insertion point.
   Right click and select **Reference**.
   When prompted for the reference length, select the left point of the bottom horizontal line, then select the right point of the bottom horizontal line to specify the existing titleblock's length.
   When prompted for the new length, enter **11"**.

   The titleblock is now re-scaled to be placed on an 8-1/2" x 11" sheet.

7. Zoom into the Firm Name and Address rectangle.

   Firm Name and Address

8. **A** Select the **MTEXT** tool.

9.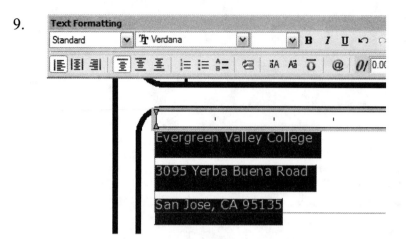

Set the Font to **Verdana**. Enter the name and address of your college.

10.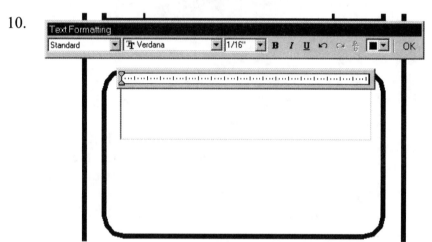

Set the text height to 1/16″. Extend the ruler to change the width of your MTEXT box to fill the rectangle.

11.
Firm Name and Address
**Evergreen Valley College**
3095 Yerba Buena Road
San Jose, CA 95135

Use **MOVE** to locate the text properly.

## Inserting a Logo

12.

| Insert | Format | Express | Design |
| --- | --- | --- | --- |

DesignCenter      CTRL

Multi-View Block...

Block...

DWG Reference...

DWF Underlay...

DGN Underlay...

Raster Image Reference...

Field...

Table...

Go to **Insert→Raster Image Reference**.

13.

**Evergreen Valley College**
3095 Yerba Buena Road
San Jose, CA 95135

Locate and select the image of your choice. (You can download *evc-logo.jpg* from www.schroff1.com.

Place the image in the rectangle.

---

**TIP:** If you are concerned about losing the link to the image file (for example, if you plan to email this file to another person), you can use **Insert→OLE Object** to embed the image into the drawing.

---

## Add a Hyperlink

14. Select the image.
Right click and select **Properties**.

15. 

Raster Image

DOCUMENTATION
Hyperlink
Notes
Reference ... (0)

Select the **Extended** tab.
Pick the Hyperlink field.

16. 

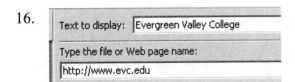

Text to display: Evergreen Valley College

Type the file or Web page name:

http://www.evc.edu

Type in the name of the school in the **Text to display** field.
Type in the website address in the **Type the file or Web page name** field.

Press **OK**.

Close the Properties dialog.

---

**TIP:** If you are unsure of the web address of the website you wish to link, use the Browse for **Web Page** button.

Browse for:

File...

Web Page...

17.

**Evergreen Valley College**
3095 Yerba Buena Road
San Jose, CA 95135

To turn off the image frame/boundary:

Type **IMAGEFRAME** at the command line.
Enter **2**.

---

**TIP:** ADT 2006 introduced a new option for IMAGEFRAME.
    0: Turns on the image frame and plots
    1: Turns off the image frame
    2: Turns on the image frame, but does not plot

---

18.

Drafter     Sheet

Date

Scale

Change the text for Project to
**Drafter**.
To change, simply double click on
the text and an edit box will appear.

19. Select the **Define Attribute** tool.

20. Select the **Field** tool.

21.

Field names:
Author
Comments
CreateDate
CurrentSheetCustom
CurrentSheetDescription
CurrentSheetNumber
CurrentSheetNumberAndTi

Format:
(none)
Uppercase
Lowercase
First capital
Title case

Highlight Author and Uppercase.

Press **OK**.

22.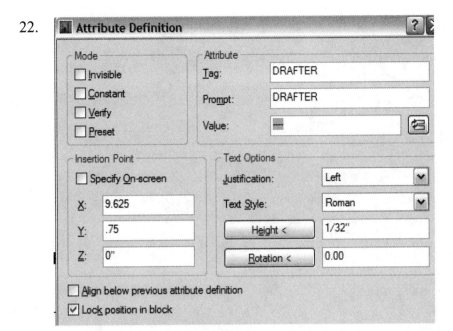

In the Tag field, enter **DRAFTER**.
In the Prompt field, enter **DRAFTER**.
The Value field is used by the FIELD property.
In the Insertion Point area:
    In the X field, enter: **9.625″**.
    In the Y field, enter: **0.75″**.
    In the Z field, enter: **0″**.
In the Text Options area:
    Set the Justification to **Left**.
    Set the Text Style to **Roman**.
    Set the Height to **1/32″**.

Press **OK**.

23.

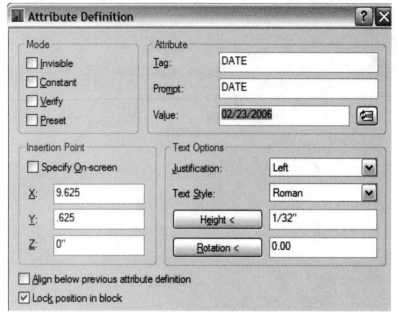

    Select the **Define Attribute** tool.

In the Tag field, enter **DATE**.
In the Prompt field, enter **DATE**.

In the Insertion Point area:
    In the X field, enter: **9.625″**.
    In the Y field, enter: **5/8″**.
    In the Z field, enter: **0″**.
In the Text Options area:
    Set the Justification to **Left**.
    Set the Text Style to **Roman**.
    Set the Height to **1/32″**.

24.   Select the Field button to set the default value for the attribute.

Select **Date**.

Set the Date format to **MM/dd/yyyy** by typing in the format field.

Press **OK**.

25.

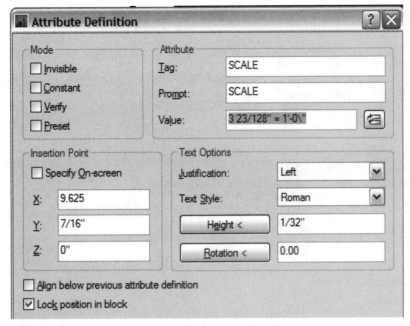

 Select the **Define Attribute** tool.

In the Tag field, enter **SCALE**.
In the Prompt field, enter **SCALE**.
In the Insertion Point area:
    In the X field, enter: **9.625″**.
    In the Y field, enter: **7/16″**.
    In the Z field, enter: **0″**.
In the Text Options area:
    Set the Justification to **Left**.
    Set the Text Style to **Roman**.
    Set the Height to **1/32″**.

26.

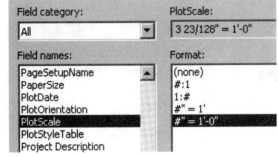

Select the Field button to set the default value for the attribute.

Select **PlotScale**.
Set the format to **#″=1′-0″**.

Press **OK**.

Press **OK** to place the attribute.

27.

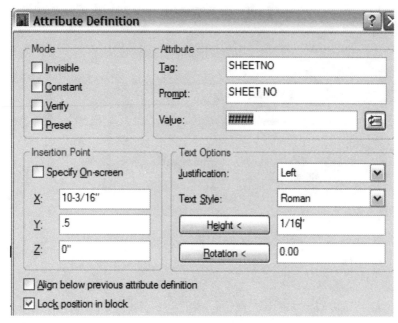

 Select the **Define Attribute** tool.

In the Tag field, enter **SHEETNO**.
In the Prompt field, enter **SHEET NO**.
In the Insertion Point area:
    In the X field, enter: **10 3/16″**.
    In the Y field, enter: **0.5**.
    In the Z field, enter: **0**.
In the Text Options area:
    Set the Justification to **Left**.
    Set the Text Style to **Roman**.
    Set the Height to **1/16″**.

28.

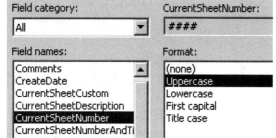

Select the Field button to set the default value for the attribute.

Select **CurrentSheetNumber**.
Set the format to **Uppercase**.

Press **OK**.

Press **OK** to place the attribute.

29.

| Mode | Attribute | | |
|---|---|---|---|
| ☐ Invisible | Tag: | PROJECTNAME | |
| ☐ Constant | Prompt: | PROJECT NAME | |
| ☐ Verify | Value: | #### | |
| ☐ Preset | | | |

| Insertion Point | Text Options | | |
|---|---|---|---|
| ☐ Specify On-screen | Justification: | Left ▼ | |
| X: 9.6 | Text Style: | Roman ▼ | |
| Y: 1.40 | Height < | 1/16" | |
| Z: 0" | Rotation < | 0 | |

 Select the **Define Attribute** tool.

In the Tag field, enter **PROJECTNAME**.
In the Prompt field, enter **PROJECT NAME**.
In the Insertion Point area:
    In the X field, enter: **9.6.**
    In the Y field, enter: **1.40.**
    In the Z field, enter: **0.**
In the Text Options area:
    Set the Justification to **Left**.
    Set the Text Style to **Roman**.
    Set the Height to **1/16″**.

30.

| Field category: | Subject: |
|---|---|
| Document ▼ | BROWN RESIDENCE |
| **Field names:** | **Format:** |
| Author | (none) |
| Comments | Uppercase |
| Filename | Lowercase |
| Filesize | First capital |
| HyperlinkBase | Title case |
| Keywords | |
| LastSavedBy | |
| Subject | |
| Title | |

Select the Field button to set the default value for the attribute.

Select **Subject**.
Set the format to **Uppercase**.

Press **OK**.

Press **OK** to place the attribute.

 **TIP:** A common error for students is to forget to enter the insertion point. The default insertion point is set to 0,0,0. If you don't see your attributes, look for them at the lower left corner of your title block and use the **Move** tool to position them appropriately.

Your titleblock should look similar to the image shown.

If you like, you can use the **Move** tool to reposition any of the attributes to make them fit better.

Do not worry about the fact that the DRAFTER attribute is too long as you only have three initials in the value field.

31.  Save the file and go to **File→Close**.

*Exercise 7-5:*
## *Creating a Drawing Template*

Drawing Name:      Architectural Title Block-Asize.dwg.
Estimated Time:    30 minutes

This exercise reinforces the following skills:

- ❑  Drawing Templates
- ❑  Insert Block

1.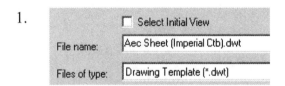

Select the **Open file** tool.

Set your Files of type: to *Drawing Template.*
Select the *Aec Sheet (Imperial Ctb).dwt.*

Press **Open.**

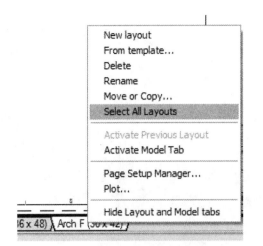

Place the cursor over the Arch F layout tab.

Right click and select **Select All Layouts**.

Hold down the Control key and select the Arch A layout.

This will make all the layouts selected EXCEPT for the Arch A layout tab.

2.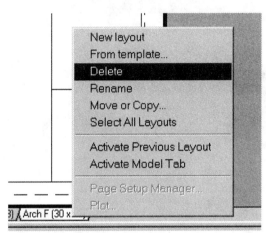

Right click and select **Delete**.

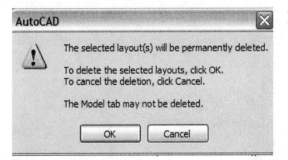

Press **OK**.

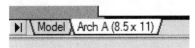

You should now have only two tabs – Model and Arch A.

Select the **Arch A** layout tab.

3.  Select the title block and the fields.
    Erase all the objects.

4.  Select the **Insert Block** tool.

5.
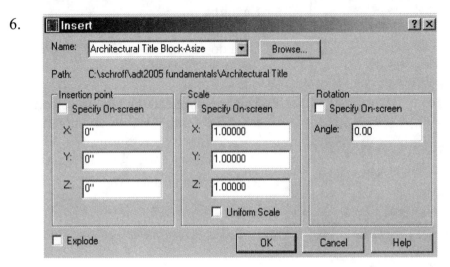

Locate the title block you created in the previous exercise.

Press **Open**.

6.

Set the Insertion point to 0,0,0.
Set the Scale to 1.0
Set the Rotation angle to 0.
Disable Explode.
Press **OK**.

7.   The attribute dialog will appear.
Press **OK**.

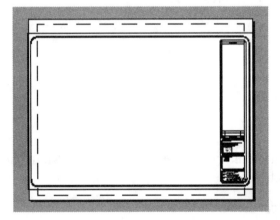

8.   Position the titleblock on the sheet layout.

## Accessing Page Setup

9.   The dotted lines on the sheet indicate the margin.
You may notice that the margin cuts off part of the titleblock.

10. 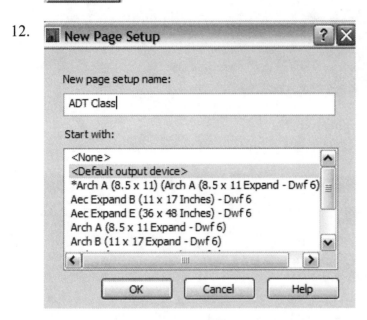 Place your mouse over the layout tab. Right click and select **Page Setup Manager**.

11. Select **New**.

12. Enter **ADT Class** for the New page setup name.

Highlight **<Default output device>** to select the printer you would normally use.

Press **OK**.

13.

The default plotter is listed.

Select the **Properties** button.

14.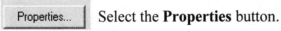

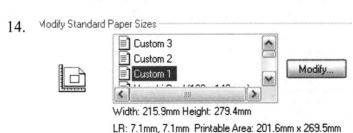

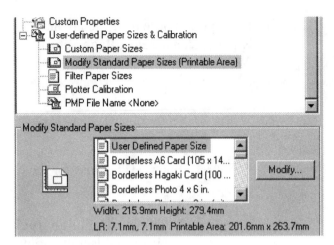

Select Modify Standard Paper Sizes (Printable Area).
Select User Defined Paper Size or Custom 1.
*(It may be different depending on the printer type.)*

Select **Modify**.

15.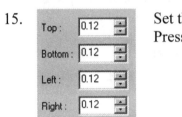

Set the Margins to **0.12**.
Press **Next**.

16. PMP File name :

ADT Class

Name the PMP File name **ADT Class**.
Press **Next**.

17. Press **Finish**.

18.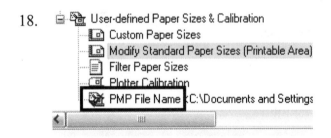

Note that the PMP File Name is set to the file you just created.

Press OK.

19. Select **Custom Properties**.

20. Enable **Landscape**.

Press **OK**.

21.   Press **OK**.

22.   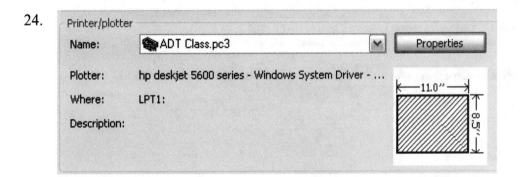   Save changes to a file named *ADT Class.pc3*.

Press **OK**.

23.   Note that the Page setup is set to ADT Class.

Page setup

Name:     ADT Class

24.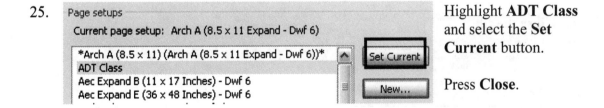

Note that the **Name** of the printer is now set to the settings you created and saved. Press **OK**.

25.   Highlight **ADT Class** and select the **Set Current** button.

Page setups

Current page setup: Arch A (8.5 x 11 Expand - Dwf 6)

*Arch A (8.5 x 11) (Arch A (8.5 x 11 Expand - Dwf 6))*
ADT Class
Aec Expand B (11 x 17 Inches) - Dwf 6
Aec Expand E (36 x 48 Inches) - Dwf 6

Set Current

New...

Press **Close**.

26. The title block now fits properly in the sheet.

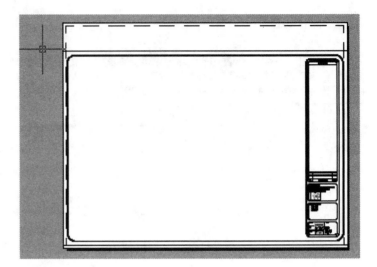

27.

Save the template in your folder with the name *Aec Sheet A.dwt*.

28. Change the description.

Press **OK**.

29. Close the file.

---

**TIP:** Use templates to standardize how you want your drawing sheets to look. Store your templates on a server so everyone in your department uses the same titleblock and sheet settings. You can also set up dimension styles and layer standards in your templates.

Keynotes are notes placed in your layout to identify materials or construction methods. ADT comes with a database of standard keynotes you can use in your layouts. In order to create or modify a keynote database, you need Microsoft Access installed on your computer. ADT comes with two types of keynotes: reference keynotes and sheet keynotes. The keynotes provided are based on the National CAD Standards (www.nationalcadstandards.org). Each keynote is defined with a keynote ID number and the actual note.

In Mechanical Engineering, keynotes are usually used to specify the tolerancing standard, the material, the finish, any silkscreen instructions, and fabrication instructions. In Architectural drafting, keynotes serve a similar purpose. They may include manufacturer instructions on how to install a window, instructions on positioning of bolts, instructions on how to seal flashing around a chimney, etc.

When you place a reference keynote, the reference number is automatically assigned, regardless of what sheet it is placed on. Sheet keynotes reference the current sheet number.

### Exercise 7-6:
## Creating a Keynote Database

Drawing Name:     AecKeynotes-Template.mdb
Estimated Time:   20 minutes

This exercise reinforces the following skills:

- ❑   Using Microsoft Access
- ❑   Keynote Databases

1.   AutoCAD Architecture comes with a template database you can use as the starting point for your own custom keynote database.

In order to complete this exercise, you need to have Microsoft Access installed. If you do not have Microsoft Access, you can download the database file from the publisher's website.

In Windows Explorer, browse to *C:\Documents and Settings\All Users\Application Data\Autodesk\ADT 2007enu\Template\Details and Keynotes.*

2.

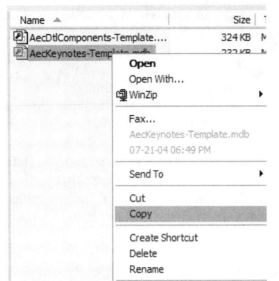

Select the *AecKeynotes-Template.mdb* file.

Right click and select **Copy**.

Browse to the folder where you are working. Right click and select **Paste**.

3.

Locate the copied database file. Right click and select **Rename**.

4.

Rename the file to *AecKeynotes-Custom.mdb*.

5.

Select the *AecKeynotes-Custom.mdb* file and press **Open**.

6.

    Create table in Design view
    Create table by using wizard
    Create table by entering data
    Fingerprint
    Groups
    KEYNOTES
    KeySort
    KEYSORTMASK

You see that Fingerprint, Groups, keynotes, KeySort, and KEYSORTMASK tables have already been defined.

7.

Highlight the Fingerprint group.
Right click and select **Open**.

The Fingerprint table identifies the keynote database and contains five fields:

| GUID | The GUID (Global Unique Identifier) is a unique ID assigned to the keynote database. You do not need to fill in this field. It will automatically be filled in when you load the database. |
|---|---|
| TYPE | This must contain the word **Keynote**. (If you are defining a detal component database, then this field must hold the word **Component**.) |
| Author | The name of the database creator |
| DisplayName | This is the name of the database that will be displayed in the dialogs. |
| Description | A description of the database contents (this is an optional field) |

8.

**Fingerprint : Table**

| GUID | Author | ID | Type | DisplayName | Description |
|---|---|---|---|---|---|
| | Elise Moss | 1 | Keynote | Schroff | keynotes |
| | | 0 | | | |

Leave the GUID field empty.
Enter your name in the Author field.
Enter **Schroff** in the DisplayName Field.
Enter **Keynotes** in the Description field.
Close the table.
If prompted to save the changes to the table, press **OK**.

9.   Highlight **Groups**.
Right click and select **Open**.

10. The Groups table has five fields.

| | |
|---|---|
| ID | This field is a sequential number. The ID must be a unique number. Once entered, this number should not be modified. This is a mandatory field. |
| Parent | This field identifies the group that is the parent of the group identified in the Group field. |
| Group | This field identifies a particular division, group, or subgroup. The groups are defined by the CSI Standard. |
| Description | This is the descriptive name of the group. |
| Modified | When the box is enabled, it means that the user changed the original contents. This is so when you install updates to ADT, your changes will not be overwritten. |

| ID | Parent | Group | Description | MODIFIE |
|---|---|---|---|---|
| 0 | \ - * | \ | * | ☐ |
| 1 | \ - * | A | Substructure | ☑ |
| 2 | \ - * | B | Shell | ☑ |
| 3 | \ - * | C | Interiors | ☑ |
| 4 | \ - * | D | Services | ☑ |
| 5 | \ - * | E | Equipment & Furnishings | ☑ |
| 6 | \ - * | F | Special Construction & Demolition | ☑ |
| 7 | \ - * | G | Building Sitework | ☑ |
| 0 | \ - * | | | ☐ |

11. First define the root groups – these are the top hierarchy for your keynote groups.

12.

| ID | Parent | Group | Description | MODIFIED |
|---|---|---|---|---|
| 0 | \ - * | \ | * | ☐ |
| 1 | \ - * | A | Substructure | ☑ |
| 2 | \ - * | B | Shell | ☑ |
| 3 | \ - * | C | Interiors | ☑ |
| 4 | \ - * | D | Services | ☑ |
| 5 | \ - * | E | Equipment & Furnishings | ☑ |
| 6 | \ - * | F | Special Construction & Demolition | ☑ |
| 7 | \ - * | G | Building Sitework | ☑ |
| 12 | B - Shell | B30 | Roofing | ☑ |
| 13 | C - Interiors | C10 | Interior Construction | ☑ |
| 37 | B - Shell | B2010 | Exterior Walls | ☑ |
| 38 | C - Interiors | C1020 | Interior Doors | ☑ |
| 43 | E - Equipment & Furnishings | E1090 | Other Equipment | ☑ |
| 155 | B - Shell | B2034 | Overhead Doors | ☑ |
| 171 | B - Shell | B3016 | Gutters & Downspouts | ☑ |
| 196 | C - Interiors | C2011 | Regular Stairs | ☑ |
| 0 | \ - * | | | ☐ |

Fill in the fields as shown.
Keep the Parent field blank.

13.

Save the Groups table.

You can now access the drop-down list under Parent to assign the correct group to each Parent.

Save again and close the table.

14. Highlight **KEYNOTES**.
Right click and select **Open**.

The Keynotes table has five fields:

| ID | This is a unique, sequential number that identifies the row number. This number should not be changed. The Keynote ID is linked to the GUID of the database. |
|---|---|
| Parent Group | This field identifies the parent group of the keynote. |
| Key | This field specifies the value from the Group field. |
| Note | This is the actual text for your keynote |
| Modified | When the box is enabled, it means that the user changed the original contents. This is so when you install updates to ADT, your changes will not be overwritten. |

15.

| ID | Parent Group | Key | Note | MODIFIED |
|---|---|---|---|---|
| 12 | B-Shell | B30.A1 | Wood Shake | ☑ |
| 62 | B-Shell | B2010.B46 | 8" CMU Wall 1.5" Rigid Insulation 2" Air 4" Brick-Soldier Course | ☑ |
| 77 | E-Equipment & Furnishin₁ | E1090.A1 | Fireplace with Chimney Brick- Soldier Course | ☑ |
| 141 | B-Shell | B2020.A2 | Arched Picture Window | ☑ |
| 186 | B-Shell | B2020.B1 | 2'-10" x 4'-10" Single Casement | ☑ |
| 193 | B-Shell | B2020.B3 | Double Casement | ☑ |
| 375 | C-Interiors | C1010.C4 | 4" Stud Partition 5/8" Gypsum Both Sides | ☑ |
| 393 | C-Interiors | C1020.A1 | Single Hinged Door | ☑ |
| 419 | C-Interiors | C1020.C1 | Single Bifold Door | ☑ |
| 0 | \-* | | | ☐ |

Fill in the fields as shown.
The Parent Group uses the drop-down list you created in the Groups Table.
The Key field allows you to enter data.
The Note field is the actual text for your note.
Be sure to enable the Modified field.

Save and close.

16.  Highlight the **KeySort** table.
Right click and select **Open**.

| ID | LENGTH | DELIMITER | PADLEFT |
|---|---|---|---|
| 0 | | | ☐ |

This table allows you to control the way keynotes are sorted for display in the Select Keynote dialog box.

The KeySort table has the following fields:

| | |
|---|---|
| ID | This field has no specified length. The ID is the number used to identify the keynote, i.e. 09350.A1 (Notice that we drop the leading alpha character.) |
| LENGTH | This determines the keys on a character by character basis. This helps to make the sorting work properly. For example, we are all familiar with the way Windows will sort a sequence as follows: 1, 2, 20, 21, 22, 23, 24, 3, 31, 4....If you set the length to 2, the sorting will take the first two digits into consideration for sorting purposes. That way the keys will be sorted properly. If your highest value key is two digits, set the length to 2. If your |
| DELIMITER | This should be a period (.) as a period is used in the keynote ID. |
| PADLEFT | Enable this field to ensure that the keynotes are sorted properly. |

**TIP:** If you prefer, you do not have to create a hierarchal keynote list. Instead, use the root parent group \-* for all keynotes.

17.

| ⊞ KeySort : Table | | | |
|---|---|---|---|
| ID | LENGTH | DELIMITER | PADLEFT |
| 1 | 2 | . | ☑ |
| 0 | | | ☐ |

In the ID field, enter **1**.
In the LENGTH field, enter **2**.
In the DELIMITER field, enter a period "**.**"
Enable PADLEFT.
Save and close the table.

18.   You are now done defining your custom database.
Close Access.

*Exercise 7-7:*
## Adding a Keynote Database to a Project

Drawing Name:      ex6-6.dwg
Estimated Time:      15 minutes

This exercise reinforces the following skills:

❑   Title blocks
❑   Attributes
❑   Layouts

1.   Open *ex6-6.dwg*.

2.   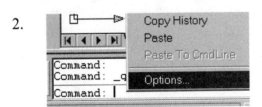 Place your cursor on the command line.
Right click and select **Options** from the shortcut menu.

3.   Select the **AEC Content** tab.

 Select the **Add/Remove** button from the Keynote Databases option.

4. 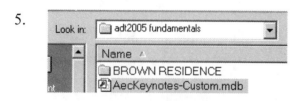   Several keynote databases have already been loaded.

   Select **Add**.

5.   Browse to your folder and select the *AecKeynotes-Custom.mdb* file that was created in the previous exercise.

6.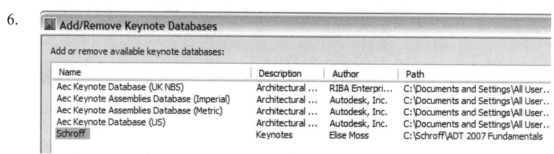

Note how the name and description are displayed.

These values were taken from the Fingerprint table you created.

7.   Highlight your custom keynote database and use the **Move Up** button to move this database to the top line on the list.

8.   Press **OK**.

9.   Press **Apply** and **OK**.

10.   Save as *ex7-7.dwg*.

11.   Close Access.

**TIP:** ADT 2005 introduced a new tool available when you are in Paper Space that allows you to quickly switch to the model space of a viewport without messing up your scale. Simply select the **Maximize Viewport** button located on your task bar to switch to model space. To switch back to paper space, select the **Minimize Viewport** button.

ADT 2005 changed the way users organizes their layouts and sheets. Starting in 2005, you use the Project Navigator to create additional drawing files with the desired views for your model. The views are created on the Views tab of the Project Navigator. You then create a sheet set which gathers together all the necessary drawing files that are pertinent to your project.

Previously, you would use external references, which would be external drawing files that would be linked to a master drawing. You would then create several layout sheets in your master drawing that would show the various views. Some users placed all their data in a single drawing and then used layers to organize the data.

This shift in the way of organizing your drawings will mean that you need to have a better understanding of how to manage all the drawings. It also means you can leverage the drawings so you can reuse the same drawing in more than one sheet set.

You can create five different types of views using the Project Navigator:

- ❑ Model Space View – a portion that is displayed in its own viewport. This view can have a distinct name, display configuration, description, layer snapshot and drawing scale.

- ❑ Detail View – displays a small section of the model, i.e. a wall section, plumbing, or foundation. This type of view is usually associated with a callout. It can be placed in your current active drawing or in a new drawing.

- ❑ Section View – displays a building section, usually an interior view. This type of view is usually associated with a callout. It can be placed in your current active drawing or in a new drawing.

- ❑ Elevation View – displays a building elevation, usually an exterior view. This type of view is usually associated with a callout. It can be placed in your current active drawing or in a new drawing.

- ❑ Sheet View – this type of view is created when a model space view is dropped onto a layout sheet.

*Note: Some classes have difficulty using the Project Navigator because they do not use the same work station each class, or the drawings are stored on a network server. In those cases, the links can be lost and the students get frustrated trying to get the correct results.*

To launch the Sheet Set Manager:

| Tools menu | Sheet Set Manager |
|---|---|
| Standard toolbar | 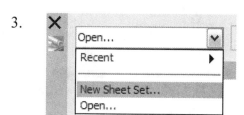 |
| Command line | sheetset |
| Shortcut key | Ctl+4 |
| Shortcut | SSM |

*Exercise 7-8:*
## Creating a Sheet Set

Drawing Name:     NEW
Estimated Time:   30 minutes

This exercise reinforces the following skills:

- ❑ Sheet Set Manager
- ❑ Layouts
- ❑ Sheets

1. Start a NEW drawing.

2. Type **SSM** to launch the Sheet Set Manager.

3.    Select the Down Arrow.

   Select **New Sheet Set**.

4.    Enable **An example sheet set**.

   Press **Next**.

5.    Highlight **New Sheet Set**.

   Press **Next**.

6.

**Name of new sheet set:**

ADT Class

**Description (optional):**

Use the New Sheet Set.dst to create a basic new sheet set without subsets, specified template or pagesetup override file.

**Store sheet set data file (.dst) here:**

C:\Schroff\ADT 2008\STUDENT FILES

Note: The sheet set data file should be stored in a location that can be accessed by all contributors to the sheet set.

☑ Create a folder hierarchy based on subsets

Sheet Set Properties

Name the sheet set **ADT Class**.

Set the **Store sheet set data file** to the class folder where you are storing your files.

Enable **Create a folder hierarchy based on subsets**.

Select the **Sheet Set Properties** button.

7.

**Sheet Creation**

| Sheet storage location | C:\Schroff\ADT 2008\STUDENT FILES |
| Sheet creation template | |
| Prompt for template | Yes |

Select the Browse button next to Sheet creation template.

8.

**Sheet Creation**

| Sheet storage location | C:\Schroff\ADT 2008\STUDENT FILES |
| Sheet creation template | Arch A (8.5 x 11)[C:\Schroff\ADT 2008\STUDENT FILES\Aec Sheet A.dwt) |
| Prompt for template | Yes |

Select the template you created as the template file to be used for you sheet set.

Press **OK**.

9.

**Sheet Creation**

| Sheet storage location | C:\Schroff\ADT 2008\STUDENT FILES |
| Sheet creation template | Arch A (8.5 x 11)[C:\Schroff\ADT 2008\ST |
| Prompt for template | No |

Set the Prompt for template to **No**.

Press **OK**.

10. Press **Next**.

11.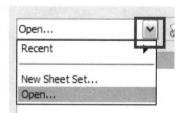

Your settings are displayed.

Press **Finish**.

12.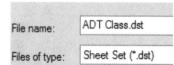

Select the Down arrow on the Sheet Set Manager.

Select **Open**.

13.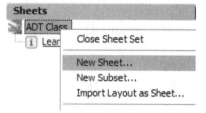

Browse to the class folder you specified.
Open the *ADT Class.dst* file.

14.

Highlight the sheet set title.

Right click and select **New Sheet**.

15.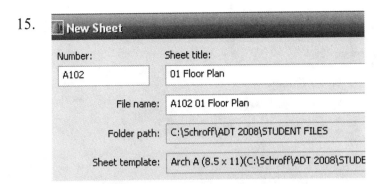

Enter **A102** in the Number field.
Enter **01 Floor Plan** as the Sheet title.
Press **OK**.

16.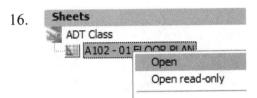

The sheet should be added to the sheet set. If it isn't, you can add it using the Import Sheet option.

Highlight the sheet.
Right click and select **Open**.

17.

Select the **Model** tab.

18.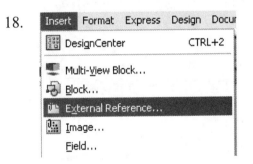

Go to **Insert→External Reference**.

19.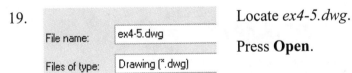

Locate *ex4-5.dwg*.

Press **Open**.

20.

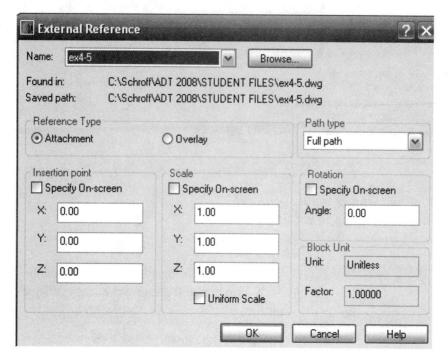

Set to insert at the origin.
Press **OK**.

21.

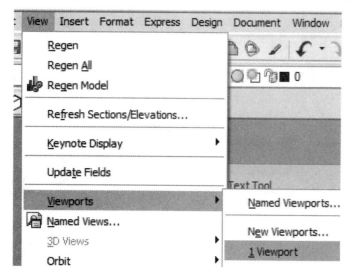

Switch to the layout tab.

22.

Go to **View→Viewports→
1 Viewport**.

23.

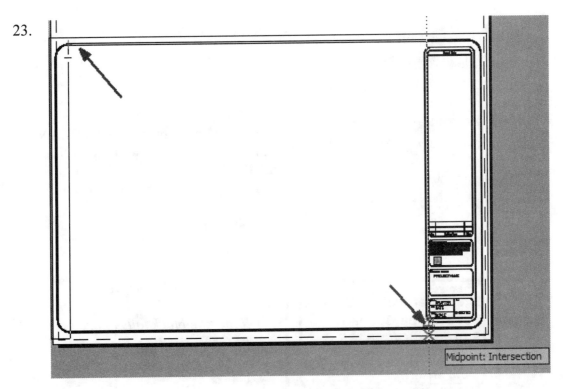

Draw a rectangle to create the viewport using the corners shown.

24.

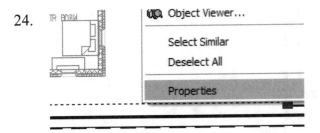

Select the viewport.
Right click and select **Properties**.

25.

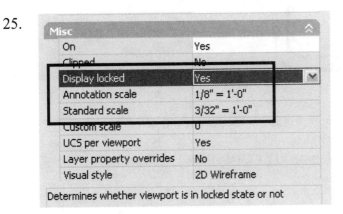

Set the Standard scale to **3/32" = 1'-0"**.

Set the Display locked to **Yes**.

*Be sure you set the scale before you lock the display or you won't be able to reset the scale.*
*By locking the display, you ensure that the display won't change even if the user zooms in and out.*

26. **Drawing Utilities**
    Drawing Properties...
    Send...

    Go to **File→Drawing Properties**.

27.
    General | Summary | Statistics | Custom

    Title:      FLOOR PLAN
    Subject:    BROWN RESIDENCE
    Author:     E. MOSS
    Keywords:

    Select the Summary tab.
    In the Title field, enter **FLOOR PLAN**.
    In the Subject Field, enter **BROWN RESIDENCE**.
    In the Author field, enter your name.

    Close the dialog.

28.

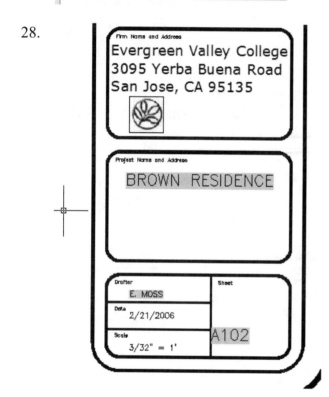

The title block updates.

*If the title block fails to update, type REGEN.*

The gray background that indicates fields can be turned on or off.

29. To turn off the gray background, type **FIELDDISPLAY** and set to **0**.

30. Save the drawing and close.

*Exercise 7-9:*
## Creating Elevation Views

Drawing Name:    ex7-7.dwg
Estimated Time:    15 minutes

This exercise reinforces the following skills:

- Creating an Elevation View
- Adding a Callout
- Named Views

1.     Open *ex7-7.dwg*.

2. Switch to the Model tab.

3.    Activate the **Top** view.

4.     Turn on the A-Roof, A-Roof-Slab, A-Door, A-Glaz, and A-Area-Mass-Grps layers.

5. 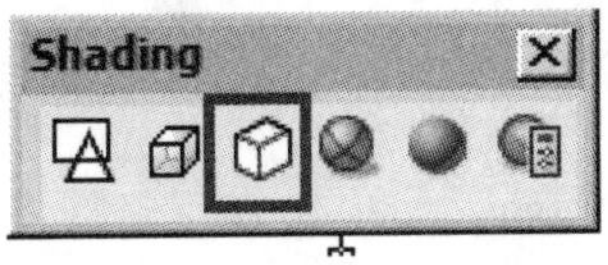    Set the view to **Hidden** mode.

6.     Use **Zoom Extents** to view the entire model.

7.     Select the Callouts Palette on the Tools Palette.
Select the **Elevation Mark A2**.

8. 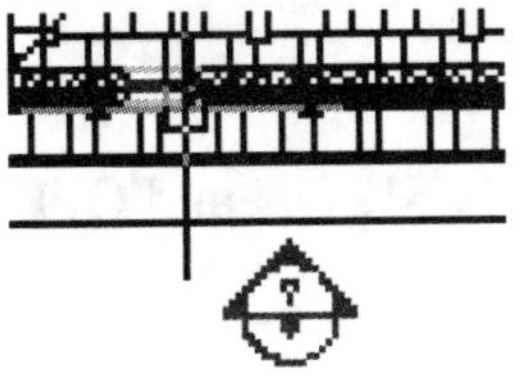    Place the elevation mark below the model.
Use your cursor to orient the arrow toward the building model.

9.

Set your view name to:
**South Elevation**.

Enable Generate
Section/Elevation.

Enable Place Titlemark.

Set the Scale to 1/8″ = 1′-0″.

Press the **Current Drawing**
button.

10. Window around the entire building to select it.
Select the upper left corner above the building and the lower right corner below the
building.

11.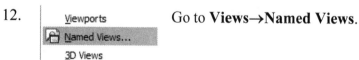

Place the elevation to the right of the
view.

Zoom into the elevation view, so you
can inspect it.

12.

Viewports
Named Views...
3D Views

Go to **Views→Named Views**.

---

**TIP:** To turn off the UCSICON, activate the viewport. Type UCSICON and OFF at
the command line. You can only turn the UCSICON OFF/ON in model space.

13.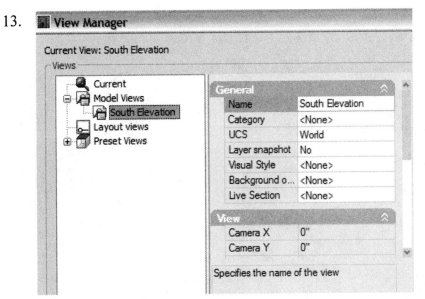

Expand the Model Views category.

The elevation is listed.

14.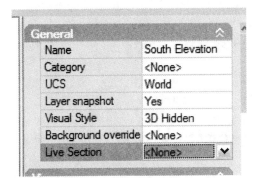

Set the Layer snapshot to **Yes**.
This saves your layer settings to this view.

Set the Visual Style to **3D Hidden**.

Press **OK**.

15.  | South Elevation |

Named views are listed in your Views toolbar.
You can activate any named view from the pull-down list.

16. Save as *ex7-9.dwg*

---

**TIP:** You can create your own custom properties by selecting the Edit Custom Properties button on the Sheet Set Properties dialog. You can then use these properties in your own fields.

Edit Custom Properties...

*Exercise 7-10:*
# Changing Hatch Patterns in an Elevation View

Drawing Name:  ex7-9.dwg
Estimated Time:  15 minutes

This exercise reinforces the following skills:

- ❑ Inserting a Titleblock
- ❑ Adding Keynotes
- ❑ Adding a Scale bar

1.  Open *ex7-9.dwg*.

2.  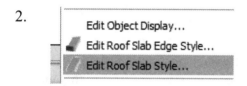 Select a roof slab on the top view.

    Right click and select **Edit Roof Slab Style**.

3.  Select the Materials tab.

    Select the **Add Material** Button.

4.  **New Material**    Name your new material **Wood Shake**.

    New Name:  Wood Shake

5.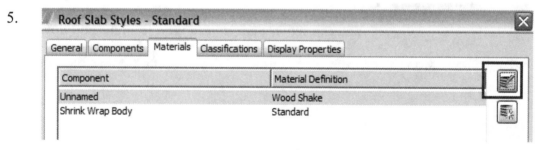

    Select the **Edit Material** button.

6.  General | Display Properties    Select the **Display Properties** tab.

7.  Select the **Properties** button.

8.

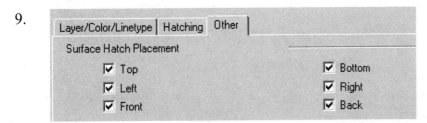

Select the Hatching tab.

Highlight all the Display Components.
Set the Hatch Pattern to **AR-RSHKE**.
Set the Scale to **3.0**.

9.

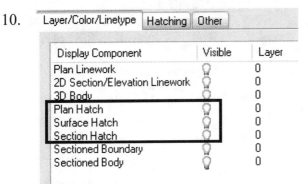

Select the Other tab.

Enable all the Surface Hatch Placement options.

10.

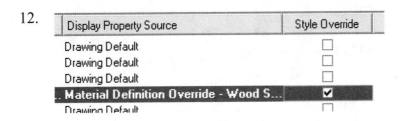

Select the Layer/Color/Linetype tab.

Turn on the layer for Plan Hatch, Surface Hatch, and Section Hatch.

11. Press **OK**.

12.

| Display Property Source | Style Override |
|---|---|
| Drawing Default | ☐ |
| Drawing Default | ☐ |
| Drawing Default | ☐ |
| **Material Definition Override - Wood S...** | ☑ |
| Drawing Default | ☐ |

Verify that the Style Override is enabled.

13. Press **OK**.

The view does not update.
It needs to be regenerated with the new definition.

14.

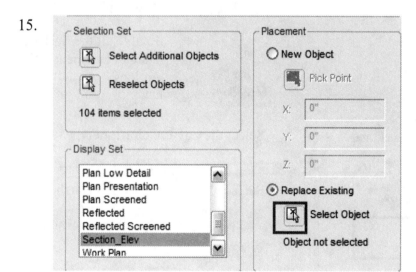

Select the elevation line in the top view.

Right click and select **Generate 2D Elevation.**

15.

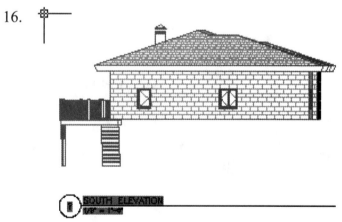

Enable **Replace Existing**.

Select the **Select Object** button.

Select the 2D Elevation placed in the previous exercise.

Press **OK**.

16.

The elevation view updates.

17. Save as *ex7-10.dwg*.

*Exercise 7-11:*
# Creating an Elevation Sheet

Drawing Name:    ex7-10.dwg
Estimated Time:    25 minutes

This exercise reinforces the following skills:

- ❏ Sheet Set Manager
- ❏ Sheet Set Properties
- ❏ Edit Drawing Properties
- ❏ Create Sheet
- ❏ Adding a View to a Sheet

1.    Go to **File→New**.

2.    
| | |
|---|---|
| File name: | Aec Sheet A.dwt |
| Files of type: | Drawing Template (*.dwt) |

Locate the template you created and select **Open**.

3.    Select the **Model** tab.

4.    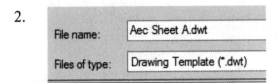

Select the **Attach XREF** tool located on the Draw toolbar flyout.

5.    
| | |
|---|---|
| File name: | ex7-10.dwg |
| Files of type: | Drawing (*.dwg) |

Select *ex7-10.dwg*.

Press **Open**.

6.

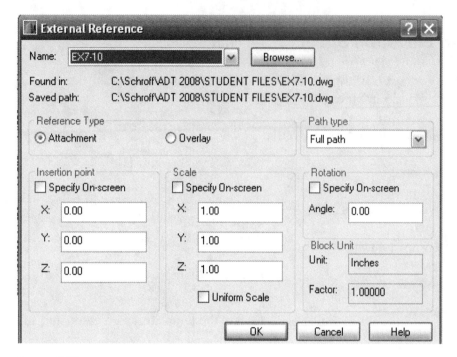

Press **OK**.

7.  Switch to the layout tab.

8.

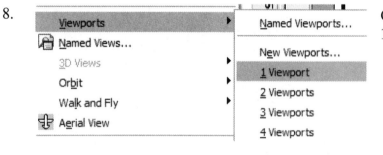

Go to **View→Viewports→ 1 Viewport**.

9.

Select two corners to place the viewport on the sheet.

Left click inside the viewport and then position the elevation view inside the viewport.

10. Select the viewport and right click, select **Properties**.

11.

| General | |
|---|---|
| Color | ■ ByLayer |
| Layer | G-Anno-Nplt |
| Linetype | ——— ByLayer |
| Linetype scale | 1.00000 |

Set the viewport on the *G-Anno-Nplt* layer.

This layer does not plot.

12.

| Misc | |
|---|---|
| On | Yes |
| Clipped | No |
| Display locked | Yes |
| Standard scale | 3/16" = 1'-0" |
| Custom scale | 0" |
| UCS per viewport | Yes |
| Visual style | 3D Hidden |
| Shade plot | Hidden |
| Linked to Sheet... | No |

Set the Standard scale to **3/16" = 1'-0"**.

Set the Shade plot to **Hidden**.

You may need to re-center the view in the viewport after you change the scale. Use PAN to do this so the scale does not change.

Lock the display.

13. Save the file as *A201  01 South Elevation.dwg*.

14. Type **SSM** to launch the Sheet Set Manager.

15.

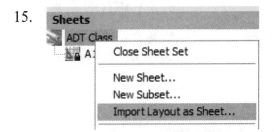

Highlight the ADT Class sheet set.

Right click and select **Import Layout as Sheet**.

16. Select drawing files containing layouts:

[ Browse for Drawings... ]

A layout can belong to only one sheet set. If a layout already belongs to a must create a copy of the layout to import it.

Select **Browse for Drawings**.

17.

File name: A201 01 SOUTH ELEVATION.dwg

Files of type: AutoCAD Drawing (*.dwg)

Select the *A201  01 South Elevation.dwg* file.
Press **Open**.

18. ☐ Prefix sheet titles with file name

Disable **Prefix sheet titles with file name**.

19. [ Import Checked ]

Select **Import Checked**.

20.

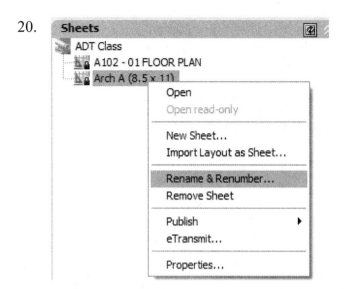

Highlight the imported sheet. Right click and select **Rename & Renumber**.

21.

In the Number field, enter **A201**.

In the Sheet title field, enter **01 SOUTH ELEVATION**.

*Note you can use the file name field to help you.*

22. Press **OK**.

23.

> Drawing Utilities
> Drawing Properties...
> Send...

Go to **File→Drawing Properties**.

24.

| General | Summary | Statistics | Custom |

Title: SOUTH ELEVATION

Subject: BROWN RESIDENCE

Author: E. MOSS

Keywords:

Enter a title, subject and author in the Summary tab.

Press **OK**.

The title block updates.

25.  Save the drawing file again.

## Adding Keynotes to a Sheet

Drawing Name:        A201 01 South Elevation.dwg
Estimated Time:      40 minutes

This exercise reinforces the following skills:

□   Adding a Keynote
□   Changing the field display

1.   Open *A201 01 South Elevation.dwg*.

2.   Select the layout tab.
     *You can stay in Paper Space mode.*

3.      Launch the Tool Palette.

     Right click on the column bar.
     Enable **All Palettes**.

4.   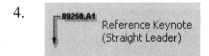   Select the Annotations Palette tab.

     Select the Reference Keynote with Leader tool.

5.
```
Command: _AecDtlAnnoLeaderAdd
Select object to keynote or ENTER to select keynote manually:
```

You'll be prompted on the command line to select an object to keynote. Select the roof slab.

The custom database you created earlier is automatically loaded.

6.
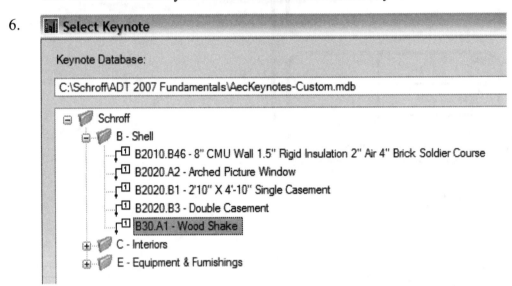

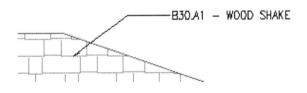  Highlight the **Wood Shake** keynote.

Press **OK**.

7.   Start the leader by selecting the roof.

B30.A1 — WOOD SHAKE

Bring the leader up and select a point for the start of the leader's shoulder.

Pick a third point for the shoulder's end.

Press Enter to accept the default text width.

8.   Select the Annotations Palette tab.

9.   Select the Reference Keynote with Leader tool.

10.
```
Command: _AecDtlAnnoLeaderAdd
Select object to keynote or ENTER to select keynote manually:
```

You'll be prompted on the command line to select an object to keynote. Select the wall.

11.

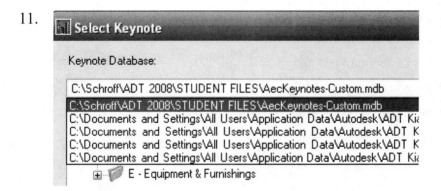

Select the custom database you loaded previously.

12.

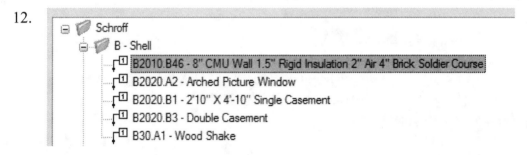

Highlight the CMU wall keynote.

Press **OK**.

13. Start the leader by selecting the wall.

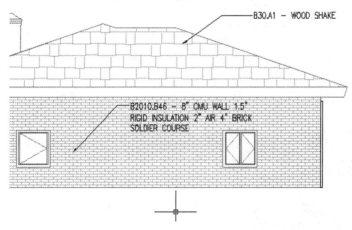

Bring the leader up and select a point for the start of the leader's shoulder.

Pick a third point for the shoulder's end.

Enter **2″** for the default text width. This will cause the keynote to wrap the text.

14. Select the Mtext.

Right click and select **MTEXT Edit**.

Repeat Move
Recent Input

Isolate Objects
Basic Modify Tools
Clipboard

AEC Modify Tools

MText Edit

15. Right click in the MTEXT dialog area.
Select **Background Mask**.

Indents and Tabs...
Bullets and Lists
Background Mask...
Justification
Find and Replace...    Ctrl+R

16. Enable **Use Background Mask**.

Set the color to **Cyan**.

Press **OK**.

Background Mask

☑ Use background mask
Border offset factor:
1.50000

Fill Color
☐ Use drawing background color    ☐ Cyan

OK
Cancel

17. Press **OK** to exit the Mtext dialog.

18. Select the Annotations Palette tab.

19. Select the Reference Keynote with Leader tool.

B9250.A1
Reference Keynote
(Straight Leader)

20.
```
Command: _AecDtlAnnoLeaderAdd
Select object to keynote or ENTER to select keynote manually:
```

You'll be prompted on the command line to select an object to keynote. Select the chimney.

21.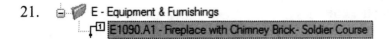

    E - Equipment & Furnishings
    ┌① E1090.A1 - Fireplace with Chimney Brick- Soldier Course

    Highlight the Fireplace keynote located under Equipment & Furnishings.

    Press **OK**.

22. Start the leader by selecting the chimney.

    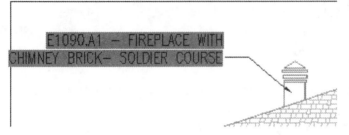

    Bring the leader up and select a point for the start of the leader's shoulder.

    Pick a third point for the shoulder's end.

23. Enter **2″** for the default text width. This will cause the keynote to wrap the text.

24. Select the Annotations Palette tab.

25. 89250.A1
    Reference Keynote
    (Straight Leader)

    Select the Reference Keynote with Leader tool.

26. Command: _AecDtlAnnoLeaderAdd
    Select object to keynote or ENTER to select keynote manually:

    You'll be prompted on the command line to select an object to keynote. Select the single casement window.

27. Schroff
    B - Shell
    ┌① B2010.B46 - 8" CMU Wall 1.5" Rigid Insulatic
    ┌① B2020.A2 - Arched Picture Window
    ┌① B2020.B1 - 2'10" X 4'-10" Single Casement
    ┌① B2020.B3 - Double Casement
    ┌① B30.A1 - Wood Shake

    Highlight the single casement keynote located under Shell.

    Press **OK**.

28.  Start the leader by selecting the chimney.

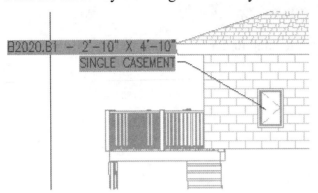

Bring the leader up and select a point for the start of the leader's shoulder.

Pick a third point for the shoulder's end.

29.  Enter **2″** for the default text width. This will cause the keynote to wrap the text.

30.  Select the Annotations Palette tab.

31.  Select the Reference Keynote with Leader tool.

32.  
```
Command: _AecDtlAnnoLeaderAdd
Select object to keynote or ENTER to select keynote manually:
```

You'll be prompted on the command line to select an object to keynote. Select the double casement window.

33.  
```
B - Shell
    B2010.B46 - 8" CMU Wall 1.5" Rigid I
    B2020.A2 - Arched Picture Window
    B2020.B1 - 2'10" X 4'-10" Single Case
    B2020.B3 - Double Casement
    B30.A1 - Wood Shake
```

Highlight the Double Casement keynote located under Shell.

Press **OK**.

34.  Start the leader by selecting the window.

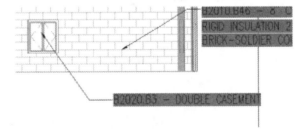

Bring the leader up and select a point for the start of the leader's shoulder.

Pick a third point for the shoulder's end.

35.  Enter **2″** for the default text width. This will cause the keynote to wrap the text.

36.

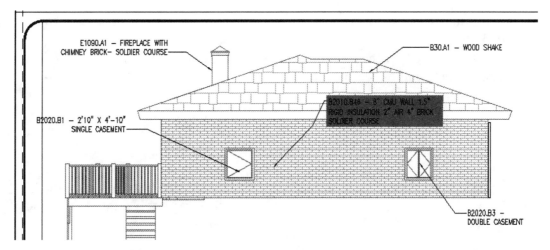

Your elevation view should be annotated properly.
Save and close.

---

**TIP:** By locking the Display you ensure your model view will not accidentally shift if you activate the viewport.

---

*Exercise 7-13:*
## Adding Elevation Labels to a Sheet

Drawing Name:      A201 01 South Elevation.dwg
Estimated Time:    10 minutes

This exercise reinforces the following skills:

- Elevation label
- Maximize Viewport
- Minimize Viewport

1.    Open *A201 01 South Elevation.dwg.*

2.    Activate model space so you can attach the elevation labels.

3.    [elevation level]    Launch the Tool Palette.
       Select the Annotation Palette.
       Locate the elevation label you created earlier.

4.    If you do not have the tool on your palette, you can add it to the palette by dragging and dropping from Windows Explorer.

5. Select the elevation label.
   Pick the right bottom of the building.
   When prompted for the rotation, enter **0**.
   The attribute edit dialog will appear.

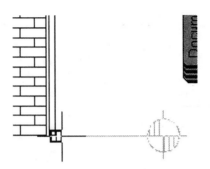

6.

   Enter **FIRST LEVEL** for the level.
   Enter **ELEV = 0'-0"** for the elevation value.

   Press **OK**.

7. Select the elevation label.
   Pick the roof edge.
   When prompted for the rotation, enter 0.
   The attribute edit dialog will appear.

   —4" BRICK 8" CM

8. 

   | LEVEL | TOP OF PARAPET |
   |-------|----------------|
   | ELEV  | elev = 8'-0"   |

   Edit the attributes.
   Change LEVEL to **TOP OF PARAPET**.
   Change ELEV to **Elev = 8'-0"**.

   Press **OK**.

   You can use the **Scale** tool to adjust the scale of the block if needed.

9. TOP OF PARAPET
   ELEV = 8'-0"

   To shift the attribute locations, pick the block and then use the grips to shift the attributes to a better location. (Turning off OSNAPS will make it easier to shift the attributes)

10.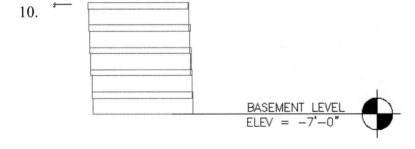

    Add an elevation label for the bottom of the stairs.

    Name the level **Basement level.**
    Set the elev to **elev = -7'-0".**

    BASEMENT LEVEL
    ELEV = −7'-0"

11. Save and close the file.

# QUIZ 4

## *True or False*

1. Columns, braces, and beams are created using Structural Members.

2. When you isolate a Layer User Group, you are freezing all the layers in that group.

3. You can isolate a Layer User Group in ALL Viewports, a Single Viewport, or a Selection Set of Viewports.

4. When placing beams, you can switch the justification in the middle of the command.

5. Standard AutoCAD commands, like COPY, MOVE, and ARRAY cannot be used in AutoCAD Architecture.

## *Multiple Choice*

6. Before you can place a beam or column, you must:

   A. Generate a Member Style
   B. Activate the Structural Member Catalog
   C. Select a structural member shape
   D. All of the above

7. Select the character that is OK to use when creating a Structural Member Style Name.

   A. -
   B. ?
   C. =
   D. /

8. Identify the tool shown.

   A. Add Brace
   B. Add Beam
   C. Add Column
   D. Structural Member Catalog

9.  Setting a Layer Key

    A.  Controls which layer AEC objects will be placed on.
    B.  Determines the layer names created.
    C.  Sets layer properties.
    D.  All of the above.

10. There are two types of stairs used in residential buildings:

    A.  INSIDE and OUTSIDE
    B.  METAL and WOOD
    C.  MAIN and SERVICE
    D.  FLOATING and STATIONARY

11. Select the stair type that does not exist from the list below:

    A.  Straight-run
    B.  M Stairs
    C.  L Stairs
    D.  U Stairs

12. The first point selected when placing a set of stairs is:

    A.  The foot/bottom of the stairs.
    B.  The head/top of the stairs
    C.  The center point of the stairs
    D.  Depends on the property settings

**ANSWERS:**

1) T; 2) F; 3) T; 4) T; 5) F; 6) D; 7) A; 8) A; 9) A; 10) C; 11) B; 12) D

## Lesson 8
# Dimensioning

We can create the best 3D model in the world, but if we cannot produce working 2D drawings that can be read by a contractor or builder, then we have not done our job.

The AIA has established a set of rules for drawings, including how sheets are to be numbered, colors, and dimensioning standards.

Drawing Annotation includes

- Dimensions
- Notes
- Schedules
- Symbols

Prior to annotation being placed, you need to set the Drawing Scale. The drawing scale determines that size of symbols and text. The command is DWGSCALESETUP.

To access the drawing scale can be accessed using **Format→Drawing Setup** and selecting the Scale tab.

---

**TIP:** The Annotation Plot Size value can be restricted by the Linear Precision setting on the Units tab. If the Annotation Plot Size value is more precise than the Linear Precision value, then the Annotation Plot Size value is not accepted.

---

Many users make the mistake of using the standard AutoCAD dimension tools to dimension their AEC objects. AutoCAD Architecture comes with a set of tools specifically for dimensioning and annotating drawings. By using these tools, dimensions and other annotations are placed on the correct layer and at the correct scale.

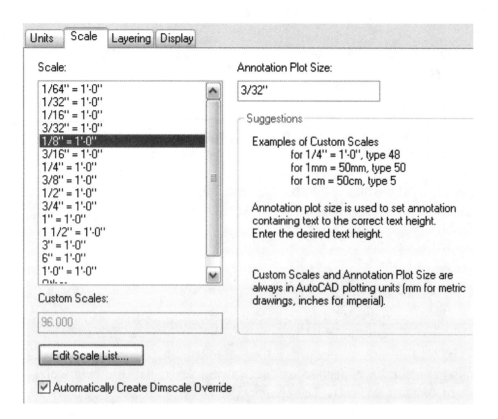

Scale-dependent objects in an Autodesk Architectural Desktop drawing are scaled automatically to reflect the units set in a drawing. Any styles that you create in metric or imperial units are scaled appropriately. You can also set the scale for the plot size of annotation in your drawing. If you are using a drawing template, then you can customize the drawing scale in your template and save the changes.

Most of the documentation tools can be accessed using the Design Center.
You simply drag and drop the desired symbol into the drawing.

*Exercise 8-1:*
# Dimensioning a Floor Plan

Drawing Name:    A102 01 Floor Plan.dwg
Estimated Time:  30 minutes

This exercise reinforces the following skills:

- Drawing Setup
- Dimension Styles
- AEC Dimensions
- Layouts

1.  Open *A102 01 Floor Plan..dwg.*

2.  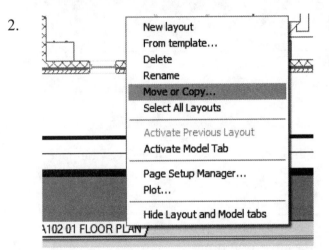  Highlight the layout tab.

    Right click and select **Move or Copy**.

3.  Enable **Create a copy**.

    Highlight **(move to end)**.

    Press **OK**.

4.  Select the second layout.

5.  Click inside the viewport to activate Model space.

6.

Select the Layer Manager.

7.

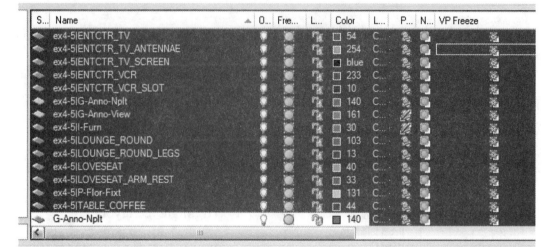

Locate the layers with the furniture and space planning entities and select.

Then select the **VP Freeze** column.

8.

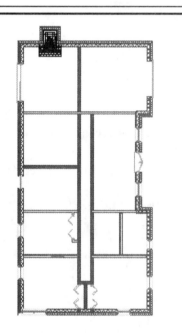

Click outside the viewport to activate paper space.

You should see the floor plan without the furniture or fixtures.

9.     Switch to the other layout and confirm that you can still see the furniture and fixtures in that layout then return to the second layout.

10. Highlight the second layout tab.

Rename
Move or Copy...
Select All Layouts

Activate Previous Layout
Activate Model Tab

Page Setup Manager...
Plot...

Hide Layout and Model tabs

AN \ A102 01 FLOOR PL...

Right click and select **Rename**.

11. n \ **A102 02 FLOOR PLAN** / Modify the layout name to **A102 02 FLOOR PLAN**.

## Add Title Mark

12. Launch the Tool Palette.

13. TITLE
    1 = 150 mm
    Select the **Title Mark** tool from the Callouts Palette.
    Pick below the view to place the title mark.

14. VIEWTITLE

    ViewportScale

    Pick two points to indicate the start and end points of the title mark.

    Place the title mark below the view.

15.
| Attribute | Text Options | Properties |
| Tag | Prompt | Value |
| --- | --- | --- |
| TITLE | Title | Floor Plan |
| SCALE | Scale | ViewportScale |

Value: 3/32" = 1'-0"

Double click to edit the attributes.
In the Scale field, enter **3/32" = 1'-0"**.
In the Title field, enter **FLOOR PLAN**.
Press **OK**.

You can apply AEC Dimensions to Walls with door and window openings and Grids.

Before you can apply AEC Dimensions, you need to check several user system options.

## ✓ Verify Dimension Settings

16. Aec-Arch-I-96 ▼ Select the **Dimension Style** tool on the Styles toolbar.

17. New... Select the **New** button.

18.

Change the Style name to **Annotative Aec-Arch-I-96**.

Set Start with to **Aec-Arch-I-96**.

Enable **Annotative**.

Set Use for: **all dimensions**.

Press **Continue**.

19.

Select the **Fit** tab.

Note that **Annotative** is enabled.

Press **OK**.

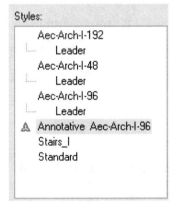

The new dimension style appears in the list. Note it has the Annotative symbol next to the name.

Current dimension style: Annotative Aec-Arch-I-96

Note that it is listed as the current dimension style.

20. 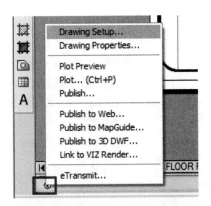 Selecting the small << arrow in the lower left corner of the screen will allow you to access **Drawing Setup**.

21. 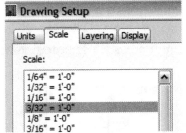 Set the Drawing Scale to **3/32" to 1'-0"**.

Press **OK**.

22. 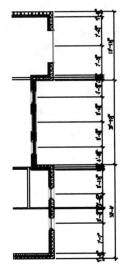 Activate the floor plan viewport by using the Maximize Viewport tool.

## Add Wall Dimensions

23. Select the **AEC Dimension (2)** tool on the Annotation Palette.

24. Add Wall Dimensions is only available in Model Space. Dimensions are automatically placed on A-Anno-Dims layer when the Layering Standard is set to AIA.

25. Window around the right side of the building to select all the walls.

Pick to the right of the building to place the dimensions.

All dimensions relevant to the wall will be placed.

26.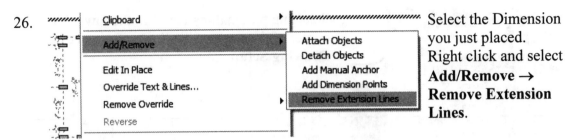

Select the Dimension you just placed. Right click and select **Add/Remove →
Remove Extension Lines**.

27. Select the extension lines for the walls that are not necessary.

The selected lines will highlight in red.

When you are done selecting, press ENTER to update the dimensions.

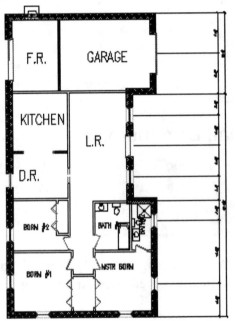

28. Minimize Viewport to return to the layout.

29. Save and close.

---

**TIP:** You can insert blocks into model or paper space. Note that you did not need to activate the viewport in order to place the Scale block.

**Lesson 9**
# Schedules

Schedules can be created to list doors, windows, walls, or any other object in your drawing. The schedule provides detail information regarding the size, construction, and vendor for each object type. Each object in a schedule is usually assigned a mark, which is placed as a tag, next to the object. Schedules form the basis of a Bill of Materials or shopping list for the contractor/builder.

The information included in the schedule is extracted from the property data attached to the drawing object (window/door/wall/etc.). Some properties are automatically generated when the object is inserted and placed in the drawing. However, other properties may be edited manually. You can also export schedule data to a .TXT file, an .XLS file or a .CSV file for use in a database. This would allow you to perform a cost analysis on required building materials.

## *Schedule Table Styles*

The format of schedule tables can be controlled using three methods:

- ❑ Use the default schedule table
- ❑ Import a style from another drawing
- ❑ Create a Custom Style

## *Using the Style Manager*

| Menu | Format →Style Manager |
| --- | --- |

The Style Manager dialog has its own toolbar and menu.

The first four icons in the dialog are standard WINDOW icons: NEW, OPEN, COPY, and PASTE. These allow users to create new styles, open an existing style, copy a style from another source, or paste from another source.

## *Edit Style*

The Edit Style button allows you to modify an existing schedule style. There are six tabs, plus a Notes and Property Sets button.

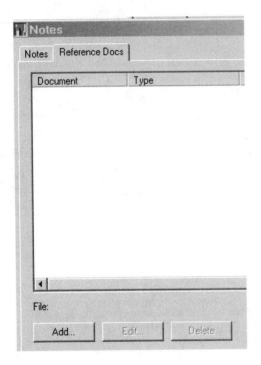

Pressing the Notes button brings up a Notes dialog box.

The user can reference specifications to support the schedule definition style or create a note to explain the schedule style.

To use an existing document, select the **Reference Docs** tab and select **Add**.

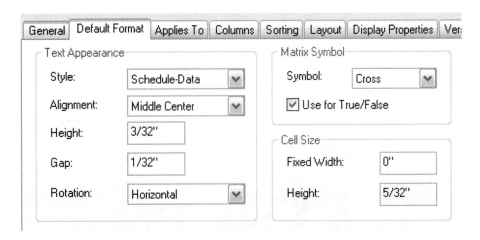

| Style | Schedule | Sets the Text Style to be used. You can assign any text style as long as it is defined and loaded. |
|---|---|---|
| | Arial-Bold<br>RomanS<br>Schedule<br>Standard | |
| Alignment | Middle Center | Sets the Alignment of the text |
| | Top Left<br>Top Center<br>Top Right<br>Middle Left | |
| Height | Sets Text Height | |
| Gap | Set the prescaled gap between the text and the schedule table lines. | |
| Rotation | Set the Rotation, which changes the text orientation within the cell. For the table title and for group titles, this option also controls the location of the cell relative to the rest of the table. | |
| Matrix Symbol | Select a Matrix Symbol, which is used by matrix displays and optionally for true/false values. | Cross<br>Check<br>Dot<br>Cross<br>Slash |
| Use for True/False | Select or clear Use for True/False to control whether matrix symbols or the data format text are used for true/false values. | |
| Cell Size | | |
| Fixed Width | Set the Fixed Width for a given column. | Specify 0.0 for widths that adjust to fit the data within them. |
| Height | Cell Size Height is a read-only field. The height is calculated from the Text Height and Gap. | |

**TIP:** The text style must be defined as an AutoCAD text style before you can apply it to the schedule table. If you want to use a different font for part of your schedule, you must first define an AutoCAD text style that uses the desired font. The text style must be loaded before it can be accessed by the Schedule Styles Manager.

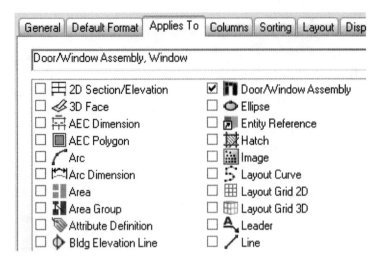

The **Applies To** tab is used to select the Objects the schedule applies to.

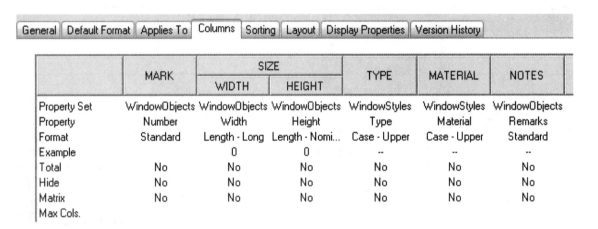

| | MARK | SIZE | | TYPE | MATERIAL | NOTES |
| | | WIDTH | HEIGHT | | | |
|---|---|---|---|---|---|---|
| Property Set | WindowObjects | WindowObjects | WindowObjects | WindowStyles | WindowStyles | WindowObjects |
| Property | Number | Width | Height | Type | Material | Remarks |
| Format | Standard | Length - Long | Length - Nomi... | Case - Upper | Case - Upper | Standard |
| Example | | 0 | 0 | -- | -- | -- |
| Total | No | No | No | No | No | No |
| Hide | No | No | No | No | No | No |
| Matrix | No | No | No | No | No | No |
| Max Cols. | | | | | | |

To add a Column, select the Add Column button.
To Add a Header, select the Add Header button.
To Modify a Column, select the Modify button.
To Delete a Column, select the Delete button.

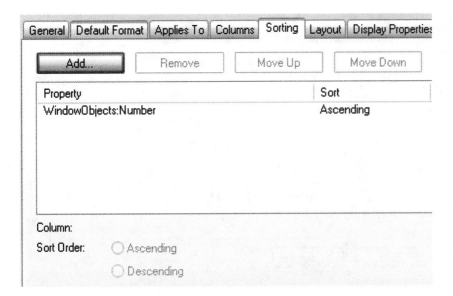

If assigned, the current property for sorting the schedule displays.

Click Add to add additional properties to sort by. The "Select Property' dialog will appear.

Select a property to sort by, and click OK. The selections presented are the columns defined on the Columns tab that are not already selected for sorting.

Select the property from the list, and then select either Ascending or Descending as the sorting method for that property.

To remove a property from the sorting list, select the property and then click Remove.

To move a property higher or lower in the sorting order, select the property and then either Move Up or Move Down.

When you finish making changes, click OK to return to the Style Manager.

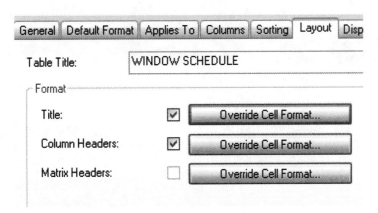

To modify the title for your schedule, click the layout tab and edit the text in the Table Title edit box.

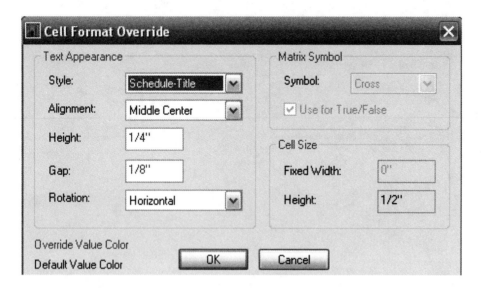

Pressing the Override Cell Format will allow you to modify the properties for each cell.

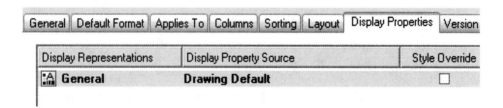

The display properties of an object affect the way the object appears in the drawing. You can override the default display for the current display configuration by setting a different visibility, layer, color, linetype, hatching, and cut plane height for the selected object.

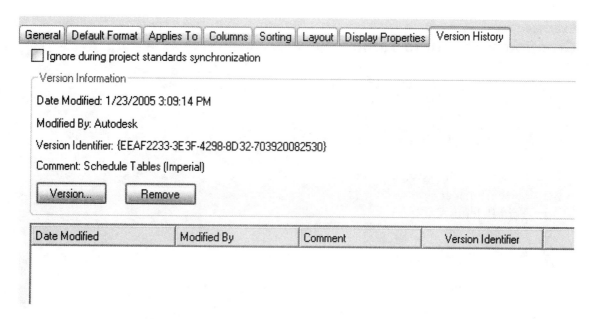

Version control allows you to document version changes of different styles.

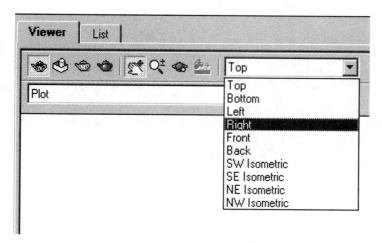

**New Style**  This icon allows the user to create a new Schedule Style. Styles are listed in alphabetical order in the style tree.

**Purge**  Purges unused schedule tables from the drawing.

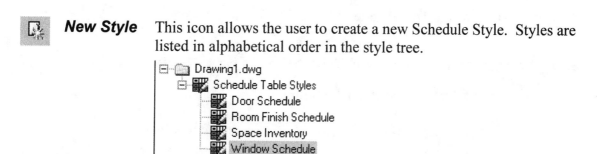

The Style Manager includes a Viewer that allows the user to change the view of the schedule that will be inserted into the drawing. You can zoom in, window, change shading, orbit, etc.

# *Creating a Schedule Table*

Drawing Name:     A102 01 Floor Plan.dwg
Estimated Time:    20 minutes

This exercise reinforces the following skills:

- ❑ Schedule Table Styles
- ❑ Style Manager
- ❑ Tool Palettes
- ❑ Layout tabs
- ❑ Layer Manager
- ❑ Viewports
- ❑ Edit Attributes

1.    Open *A102 01 Floor Plan.dwg.*

2.    Launch the Tool Palette.

3.    **Annotation**    Right click on the Palette bar.

    **Scheduling**    Select **Scheduling**.

4.    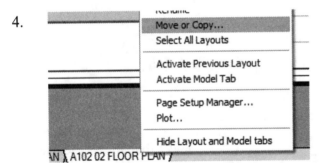    Select the 02 Floor Plan tab.

    Right click and select **Move or Copy**.

5.    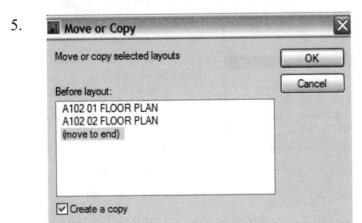    Enable **Create a copy**.

    Highlight **(move to end)**

    Press **OK**.

6. **A102 03 WINDOW SCHEDULE**    Select the new Floor Plan tab.

7. Rename the layout **A102 03 WINDOW SCHEDULE**.

8. **Window Schedule**    Select the **Window Schedule** tool from the Scheduling Palette. Drag and drop into the viewport.

9. You'll be prompted to select objects.
   Type **all**.
   This will automatically filter out all the objects except the windows to be used in the schedule.
   Press **Enter**.
   Pick a point to place the schedule.
   Press **Enter** to accept the default placement for the second point.

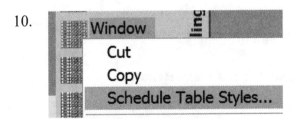

The Window Schedule is placed.

10.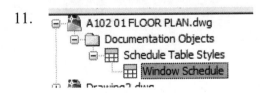

    Highlight the **Window Schedule** on the Palette.

    Right click and select **Schedule Table Styles**.

11. A102 01 FLOOR PLAN.dwg
    Documentation Objects
    Schedule Table Styles
    Window Schedule
    Drawing2.dwg

    The Window Schedule is listed in the Style Manager.

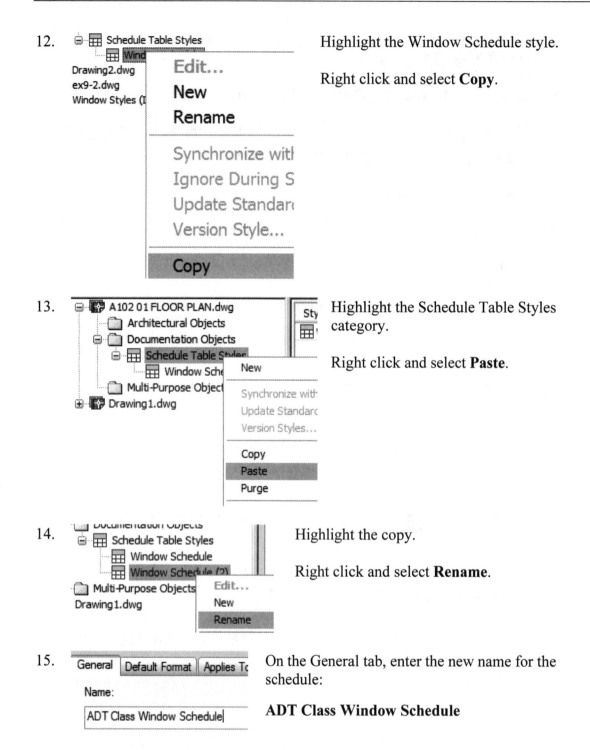

12.  Highlight the Window Schedule style.

Right click and select **Copy**.

13.  Highlight the Schedule Table Styles category.

Right click and select **Paste**.

14.  Highlight the copy.

Right click and select **Rename**.

15.  On the General tab, enter the new name for the schedule:

**ADT Class Window Schedule**

Note that the schedule list reorganizes to be in alphabetic order.

16.

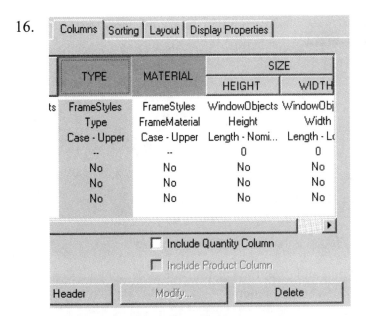

Select the Columns tab.

Select the MATERIAL column.

Select the **Delete** button.

17.

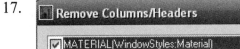

Press **OK** and close the dialog.

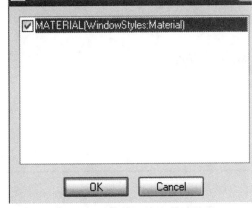

18.

Move the TYPE column by dragging and dropping it next to the MARK column.

19. Select the **Floating Viewer** tool in the lower left corner of the dialog.

20.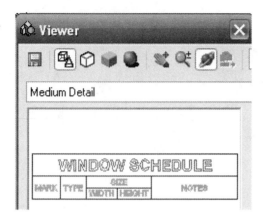

The preview window shows what the schedule will look like.

21. Save the drawing.

22.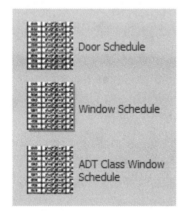

Drag and drop the Custom Window Schedule onto the Schedule Palette.

You need to save the drawing before you will be allowed to drag and drop the new schedule onto the Tool Palette.

Close the Style Manager.

23. Save and close.

**TIP:** You need to place your tags on the parent drawing where the door, window, etc. exists and not in an external reference. If you place tags in the external reference, your schedule table will not appear properly… you will see multiple iterations of each tagged item.

### Exercise 9-2:
## Adding Window Tags

Drawing Name:       A102 01 Floor Plan.dwg
Estimated Time:     10 minutes

This exercise reinforces the following skills:

❑   Schedule Tags

1.   Open *A102 01 Floor Plan.dwg.*

2.   Select the 03 Window Schedule tab.

3.   Select the **Maximize Viewport** tool.

4.   Launch the Tool Palette.

5.   Select the **Window Tag** tool from the Schedules Palette.

6.   Select each window.
     Press **ENTER** to center the tag on each window.
     Press **OK** to accept the default properties.

     *If you get an error stating that a window was not selected, just zoom in closer and re-select.*

7.   Minimize the Viewport to return to paper space.

8.   Save as *ex9-2.dwg.*
     *We will update the Window Schedule in a later exercise.*

---

 **TIP:**   The Window Tags should automatically be placed on the **A-Glaz-Iden** Layer.

*Exercise 9-3:*
## Adding Door Tags

Drawing Name:     ex9-2.dwg
Estimated Time:    15 minutes

This exercise reinforces the following skills:

- ❑ Schedule Tags
- ❑ Layout tabs
- ❑ Layer Manager
- ❑ Viewports
- ❑ Edit Attribute

1. 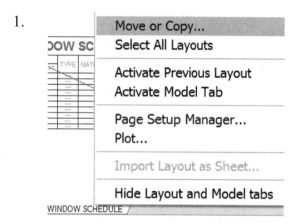 Select the **03 Window Schedule** layout tab.

   Right click and select **Move or Copy**.

2. 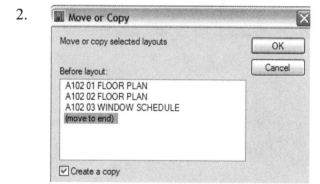 Enable **Create a copy**.

   Highlight **(move to end)**.

   Press **OK**.

3. 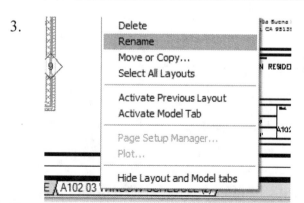 Select the new Window Schedule tab.

   Right click and select **Rename**.

4. **A102 04 DOOR SCHEDULE**

   Rename the layout **A102 04 DOOR SCHEDULE**.

5. A-Glaz-Iden
   A-Glaz-Iden
   Freeze or thaw in current viewport
   ex4-6|A-Anno-Titl
   ex4-6|A-Anno-Titl-Bdry

   Activate model space by left clicking inside the viewport.

   In the Layer Manager drop-down, select **Viewport Freeze** to freeze the A-Glaz-Iden layer.

6. P OTRACK DUCS DYN LWT PAPER

   Select the **Maximize Viewport** tool.

7. (001) Door Tag

   Select the **Door Tag** tool from the Schedules Palette.

8.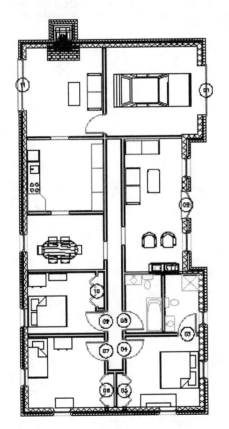

   Select each door.
   Press **ENTER** to center the tag on each window.
   Press **OK** to accept the default properties.

9. Door S...

   Verify that you are still in model space.
   Select the **Door Schedule** from the Tool Palette.

10. Type **All** at the Select Objects prompt.
    Press **Enter**.
    Click to place the schedule.
    Press **Enter**.

11.

Selection
Export...
Convert to Table

▨ Select Component

Edit Object Display...
⊞ Edit Schedule Table Style...

Select the Door Schedule.

Right click and select
**Edit Schedule Table Style**.

12. | DUCS DYN LWT | MODEL | ◄ | ▣ Minimize Viewport |

Minimize the viewport.

13. Save as *ex9-3.dwg*.

---

**TIP:** The Door Tags should automatically be placed on the **A-Door-Iden** Layer.

---

*Exercise 9-4:*

## Adding a Schedule Table

Drawing Name:      ex9-3.dwg
Estimated Time:     20 minutes

This exercise reinforces the following skills:

- Add Schedule Table
- Schedule Properties
- Viewports

1. Open *ex9-3.dwg*.

2. 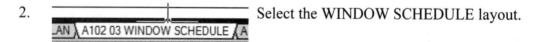    Select the WINDOW SCHEDULE layout.

3.     Select the **Maximize Viewport** tool.

4. 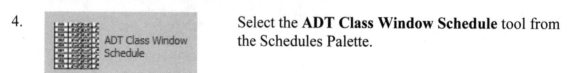    Select the **ADT Class Window Schedule** tool from the Schedules Palette.

5.

Drag and drop onto the sheet.

Custom Window
Schedule

6.

Press ENTER to schedule an external
drawing.

**WINDOW SCHEDULE**

| MARK | TYPE | SIZE | | NOTES |
|------|------|------|--------|-------|
| | | WIDTH | HEIGHT | |

Pick to place the schedule on the sheet.

7.

Edit Table Cell
Add All Property Sets
Selection
Export...

Edit Object Display...
Edit Schedule Table Sty

Copy Schedule Table S

Object Viewer...

Select Similar
Deselect All

Properties

Select the window schedule.

Right click and select **Properties**.

8.

| General | | |
|---------|---|---|
| Description | | |
| Layer | | A-Anno-Schd |
| Style | | ADT Class Windo... |
| Title | | WINDOW SCHEDULE |
| Scale | | 128.00000 |
| Update automatically | | Yes |

In the General Section:
Set Update Automatically to **Yes**.

9.

| Selection | |
|-----------|---|
| Add new objects automatically | Yes |
| Scan xrefs | Yes |
| Scan block references | Yes |
| Layer wildcard | *Glaz* |

In the Selection Section:
Set Add new objects automatically to
**Yes**.
Set Scan xrefs to **Yes**.
Set Scan block references to **Yes**.
In the Layer wildcard field, Type
**\*Glaz\***.

10. 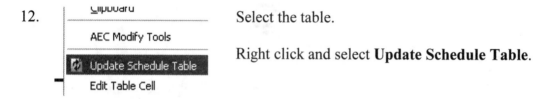 Scroll down to the **External Source** section.

Set Schedule external drawing to **Yes.**

In the External drawing field, select **Browse**.

11. Locate the *ex9-3.dwg* and press **Open**.

12. 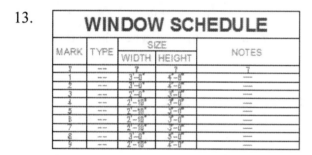 Select the table.

Right click and select **Update Schedule Table**.

13.  The schedule table updates.

14. Minimize the viewport.

15. Save as *ex9-4.dwg*.

*Exercise 9-5:*
## Exporting a Schedule

Drawing Name:    ex9-4.dwg
Estimated Time:    15 minutes

This exercise reinforces the following skills:

- ❑ Table Styles
- ❑ Creating a New Table Style
- ❑ Exporting an Exiting Schedule Table

1. Open *ex9-4.dwg.*

2. 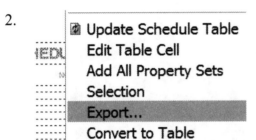 Select the window schedule.

   Right click and select **Export**.

3. 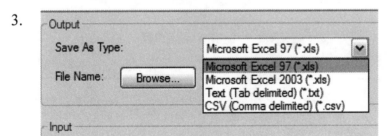 You have three options of file type you can export: Excel, text, or csv.

   Select .txt.

4. Pressing the Browse button will allow you to set the path where the export file will be saved.

5. 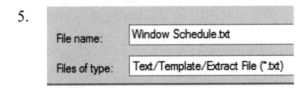 Change the file name to **Window Schedule**.
   Press **Save**.

   Press **OK**.

6. Locate the file you just created and open using Notepad.

   window
   schedule.txt

7.

```
WINDOW SCHEDULE
MARK      TYPE     WIDTH     HEIGHT    NOTES
?         --       ?         ?         ?
1         --       3'-0"     4'-6"     --
2         --       3'-0"     4'-6"     --
3         --       2'-10"    3'-0"     --
4         --       2'-10"    3'-0"     --
5         --       2'-10"    3'-0"     --
6         --       2'-10"    3'-0"     --
7         --       2'-10"    3'-0"     --
8         --       2'-10"    3'-0"     --
9         --       2'-10"    4'-10"    --
```

The file shows the data.

Close the text file.

8.  Close the AutoCAD Architecture file.

## Lesson 10
# Creating a Video

One of the more fun (and the more frustrating) tools within AutoCAD Architecture is the ability to create a video.

A video requires two basic things:

A path – this is the path, which the camera will travel along. The path must be an open or closed polyline, circle, or rectangle.

A camera – the camera can be set to point to different angles and elevations along the path.

*Exercise 10-1:*
## *Adding a Path*

Drawing Name:      Ex7-7.dwg
Estimated Time:     5 minutes

This exercise reinforces the following skills:

❑   Creating a path

1.        Open *ex7-7.dwg.*

        Model   Work     Switch to the Model tab.

2.        Switch to a top view.

3.  Draw a circle around the house.

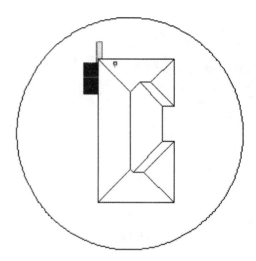

4.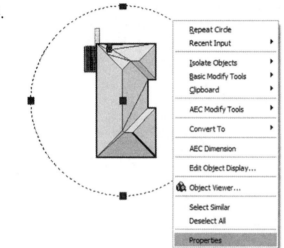

    Select the circle.
    Right click and select **Properties**.

5.  Set the Center Z to 5'-6". This changes the
    elevation of the circle.
    This will move the camera path so it is
    approximately eye level.

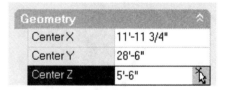

6.  Save the file as *ex10-1.dwg*.

*Exercise 10-2:*

## *Using the Camera Tool*

Drawing Name:     Ex10-1.dwg
Estimated Time:     10 minutes

This exercise reinforces the following skills:

    ❑   Adding a Camera View
    ❑   Adjust Camera View

1.     Open *ex10-1.dwg.*

2. 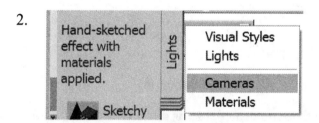    Right click on the Tool Palette.

Select **Cameras**.

3.
This camera has a 35 mm lens length. Use this camera to create wide-angle views.

Wide-angle Camera

Locate the **Wide-angle Camera** tool.
Scroll through the camera choices and notice you have three different cameras pre-set for your use.

4.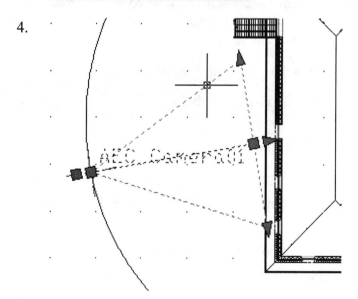

Place the camera on the circle using the NEArest snap.

With ORTHO OFF, you can direct the camera's viewpoint.

Direct the camera so it is facing the house as the target point.

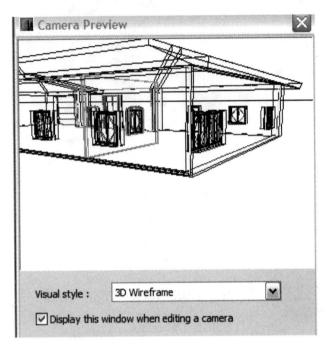

Select the Camera.

A preview window will appear so you can see what the camera sees.

5.

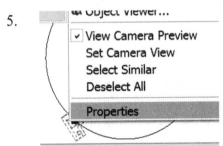

Right click and select **Properties**.

Note that you can enable or disable whether or not you get a camera preview.

6.

| Camera | |
|---|---|
| **Camera** | |
| Name | My Camera |
| Camera X | -20'-1 19/32" |
| Camera Y | -10'-9 7/8" |
| Camera Z | 5'-6" |
| Target X | 6'-7 5/8" |
| Target Y | 6'-4 19/32" |

It is important to give the camera a name so you can keep track when you want to switch from one camera to another when creating your video.

Change the name for the camera.

Close the Properties dialog.

7.

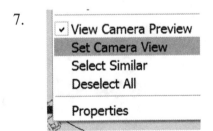

Select the camera. Right click and select **Set Camera View**.

If you have a scroll wheel on your mouse, you can use it to move your camera view closer or farther from the model.

8.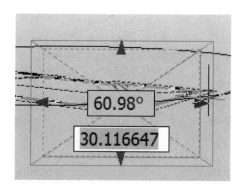

You can select one of the blue grip arrows and use it to adjust the field of view.

Watch how the view changes in the preview window as you move the arrow.

Hit ESC when you are done.

9. Experiment with different camera perspectives until you get the camera view you like.

10. Save as *ex10-2.dwg*.

**TIP:** You can use the camera grips to change the rotation, lens length, and camera position.

*Exercise 10-3:*
## Creating a Video

Drawing Name:      Ex10-2.dwg
Estimated Time:     15 minutes

This exercise reinforces the following skills:

❑   Creating a Video

1.      Open *ex10-2.dwg.*

2.   Type **ANIPATH** on the command line.

3.   Enable the Path button under Camera.

Then select the Pick button to select the camera path.

Select the circle you drew as the path.

4.   You will be asked to assign a name for the path.

Name it **My Path**.

Press **OK**.

---

**TIP:** Enable **Corner Deceleration** for the camera to move slower as it turns corners on the path.

---

5.   Enable Point under Target.

Press the select button.

Select a point approximately in the center of the house.

6.   You'll be asked to name your point.
Enter **Inside House**.
Press **OK**.

**TIP:** Selecting a regen option other than As Displayed performs a full regeneration of each frame and specifies the shading options for the AVI file generated.

7. Set the Visual Style to **Realistic**.

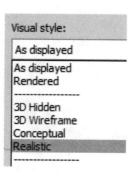

Visual style:

As displayed
------------------
As displayed
Rendered
------------------
3D Hidden
3D Wireframe
Conceptual
Realistic
------------------

8.

Animation settings

Frame rate (FPS):      25

Number of frames:     125

Duration (seconds):   5.00

Set the Frame rate (FPS) to **25**.

The Number of Frames will automatically adjust for that setting.

Set the Duration to **5.00** seconds.

9.

Format:

WMV

AVI
MOV
MPG
WMV

You can select AVI, MOV, MPG, or WMV format. MPG and WMV are preferred if you plan to create a DVD of your animation.

Since we will be playing the videos on our computers, select AVI.

10.

Resolution:

320 x 240

160 x 120
320 x 240
640 x 480
800 x 600
1024 x 768

You can select several window sizes for your animation. The larger the size selected, the larger the file size.

Select the **320 x 240**. You can always create a larger video once you see how it looks in a draft version.

11.

Preview...

You can preview your animation before you record.
Select **Preview**.

12.

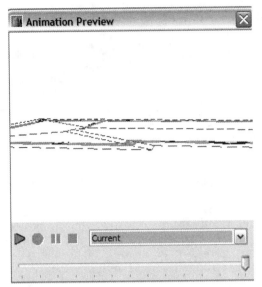

A preview window will appear. You can also watch how the camera travels along the path.

Press the Green Arrow to play the preview.

Close the preview window.

Adjust the path, pick points or camera as needed if you are not happy with the preview. The video quality of the preview is less than the final result.

13. Press **OK** on the Motion Path Animation dialog to create your video.

14.. | File name: | trial1 |
    | Files of type: | *.avi |

Browse to your work folder.
Name your video *trial1.avi* and select **Save**.

---

**TIP:** The avi format can be played using Microsoft Video Player or Real Player.

---

It will take a few minutes for the avi to be created.

A progress bar will appear to help you track how long it is taking.

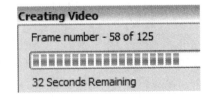

15. Save as *ex10-3.dwg*.

16. Locate the avi file in your work folder and play it.

# COMPREHENSIVE FINAL EXAM

## *True or False*

1.  Doors, windows, and stairs are inserted into a drawing as objects.
2.  The Object Viewer is a dialog box that allows you to view an object prior to placement.
3.  The handle for placing a wall is located at the bottom of the Wall Justification line.
4.  The Offset option of the Add Wall command shifts the justification handle off the justification line the Offset Value distance.
5.  Wall Grips are located at the beginning, middle, and end on the bottom of the justification line of a wall.
6.  AutoCAD commands such as OFFSET, TRIM, and EXTEND can be used to create and modify walls.
7.  You can use wall grips to copy, stretch, or move walls.
8.  Polylines can be converted to walls.
9.  Door styles can not be copied.
10. Flip Hinge can be used to change the location and swing of a door or window.
11. You can change the location of a door or window using GRIPS.
12. If you remove a door or window from a wall, it will leave a gap.  You will then need to "heal" the wall to close the opening.
13. Openings can be created with a specified width and height.
14. You can import door and window styles from external sources.
15. Roof properties define the thickness of the roof plane and the angle of the fascia.
16. The angle of a roof can be defined by the ratio of the rise to run or by a slope angle.
17. The CONVERT TO ROOF command is used to create a roof from a roof slab.
18. The ADDRAILING command can place a railing attached to stairs ONLY.
19. The scale for symbols and annotation is set with the OPTIONS dialog.
20. The Create AEC Content Wizard can be used to create a tool for a Tool Palette.
21. The Model Explorer allows you to view mass groups and elements.
22. The Model Explorer allows you to name mass groups and elements.
23. Grouping Mass Elements is the same as Joining them together.
24. A camera can be used to obtain views of a building.
25. In order to create a video, you must create a path.

## *Multiple Choice*

1. The Menu Group that includes AutoCAD Architecture toolbars is:

    A. ACAD
    B. ACCOV
    C. ADT
    D. EXPRESS

2. To launch the Tool Palette, press:

    A. Ctl+2
    B. Ctl+3
    C. Shift+2
    D. Shift+3

3. To launch the Design Center, press:

    A. Ctl+2
    B. Ctl+3
    C. Shift+2
    D. Shift+3

4. To freeze all layers except those layers in a Layer User Group, use:

    A. Isolate User Group
    B. Filter User Group
    C. Quick Select
    D. Freeze Invert User Group

5. The default layer standard for the Imperial template is:

    A. None
    B. AIA (256 Colors)
    C. Generic AutoCAD Architecture
    D. Standard

6. The limits of the AEC_Arch Imperial templates is set to this by default:

    A. 1′, 9′
    B. 288′-0″,192′-0″
    C. 144′-0″, 96′-0″
    D. None of the above

7. The default scale factor for symbols and dimensions of the AEC_Arch Imperial template is:

    A. ¼″ = 1′
    B. ½″ = 1′
    C. 1″ = 1′
    D. 1/8″ = 1′

8. Walls have all of the following properties EXCEPT:

    A. Width
    B. Height
    C. Justification
    D. Thickness

9. The command to Convert a Polyline to a Wall is:

    A. WALLCONVERT
    B. POLYLINECONVERT
    C. CONVERT
    D. WALLPROPS

10. Select the entity type that CAN NOT be converted to a wall:

    A. LINE
    B. POLYLINE
    C. SPLINE
    D. ARC

11. The command to insert a Door into a drawing is:

    A. DOORADD
    B. ADDDOOR
    C. INSERT
    D. DOORINSERT

12. The Style of a door is defined using this command:

    A. DOORSTYLE
    B. STYLEDOOR
    C. DOORTYPE
    D. STYLETYPE

13. A single hinged door will display at an angle of 90 degrees if the opening percent is set to:

    A. 90
    B. 50
    C. 25
    D. 0

14. The _____ of an Arch Window defines its radius.

    A. RADIUS
    B. RISE
    C. HEIGHT
    D. DIAMETER

15. Roofs are created with the command:

    A. ADDROOF
    B. ROOFADD
    C. INSERT
    D. INSERTROOF

16. The following entity type CAN NOT be used by the CONVERT TO ROOF command:

    A. Roof slab
    B. Line
    C. Polyline
    D. Walls

17. The command to insert stairs into a drawing is:

    A. STAIRADD
    B. ADDSTAIR
    C. INSERT
    D. INSERTSTAIRS

18. Straight stairs are created using this Shape setting:

    A. Multi-Landing
    B. Spiral
    C. Straight
    D. U-Shaped

19. The Shape options for stairs include all those listed below EXCEPT:

    A. U-SHAPED
    B. Multi-Landing
    C. Floating
    D. Straight

20. To launch the Autodesk Content Browser, use:

    A. Ctl+2
    B. Ctl+3
    C. Ctl+4
    D. Ctl+5

21. Setting the Drawing Scale establishes the _____ of dimensions.

    A. units
    B. text height
    C. text style
    D. placement

22. Mass Elements can be created using the _____ Command:

    A. MassElementAdd
    B. ElementAdd
    C. MassAdd
    D. None of the above

23. Mass Elements are placed on this layer (using the AIA standard):

    A. A-AREA-MASS
    B. A-SOLIDS
    C. A-ELEMENTS
    D. A-MASS-ELEMENT

24. Which components make up the display system in AutoCAD Architecture?

    A. Scale, objects, and linetype settings.
    B. The viewports, layer settings, and scale.
    C. The plotscale, objects, and linetype settings.
    D. A viewport, objects, and a viewing direction for the objects.

25. What does the priority for components represent when creating or modifying wall styles?

    A. Importance values for use in wall cleanup at intersections.
    B. Relative structural strength values for the components of the wall style.
    C. Priority controls the display order of the individual wall components for the style.
    D. The assembly order of the individual wall components for construction purposes.

**ANSWERS:**

**True-False**
1) T; 2) T; 3) T; 4) T; 5) T; 6) T; 7) T; 8) T; 9) F; 10) T; 11) T; 12) F; 13) T; 14) T; 15) T; 16) T; 17) F; 18) F; 19) F; 20) T; 21) T; 22) T; 23) F; 24) T; 25) F

**Multiple Choice**
1) C; 2) B; 3) A; 4) A; 5) B; 6) B; 7) D; 8) D; 9) A; 10) C; 11) A; 12) A; 13) B; 14) B; 15) B; 16) A; 17) A; 18) C; 19) C; 20) C; 21) B; 22) A; 23) A; 24) B; 25) A

## About the Author

Elise Moss has worked for the past twenty years as a mechanical designer in Silicon Valley, primarily creating sheet metal designs. She has written articles for Autodesk's Toplines magazine and AUGI's PaperSpace. She is President of Moss Designs, creating custom applications and designs for corporate clients. She has taught at DeAnza College, Evergreen Valley College and San Francisco State University. She holds a BSME from San Jose State University.

She has been married more than twenty-five years to Ari Stassart, a computer scientist. They have three sons. Benjamin is an electrical engineer at a small firm in Silicon Valley. Daniel is a project manager for a local construction firm. Isaiah is still in elementary school.

She can be contacted via email at elise_moss@mossdesigns.com

More information about the author and her work can be found on her website at www.mossdesigns.com.

**NOTES:**

**NOTES:**

**NOTES:**